WEST YORKSHIRE VOL I

Edited by Annabel Cook

First published in Great Britain in 2003 by
YOUNG WRITERS
Remus House,
Coltsfoot Drive,
Peterborough, PE2 9JX
Telephone (01733) 890066

SB ISBN 1 84460 256 7

FOREWORD

Young Writers was established in 1991 as a foundation for promoting the reading and writing of poetry amongst children and young adults. Today it continues this quest and proceeds to nurture and guide the writing talents of today's youth.

From this year's competition Young Writers is proud to present a showcase of the best poetic talent from across the UK. Each hand-picked poem has been carefully chosen from over 66,000 'Hullabaloo!' entries to be published in this, our eleventh primary school series.

This year in particular we have been wholeheartedly impressed with the quality of entries received. The thought, effort, imagination and hard work put into each poem impressed us all and once again the task of editing was a difficult but enjoyable experience.

We hope you are as pleased as we are with the final selection and that you and your family will continue to be entertained with *Hullabaloo! West Yorkshire Vol I* for many years to come.

CONTENTS

Joseph Lawton (10)   1
Marya Hussain (9)   1
Natalie Hirst (9)   2
Gemma Pearce (9)   2

Christ Church (VA) Junior School
Joshua Vickers (11)   3
Katie Whitehead (11)   3
Lisa Doyle (11)   4
Charlotte Balmforth (11)   5
Shane Dow (11)   6
Sophie Whitehead (11)   7

Collingham Lady Hastings CE Primary School
Natalie Mawer (9)   7
Lizzy Quirke (10)   8
Katherine Duncan (8)   8
Kizzy Strodder (9)   9
Caroline Simpson (10)   9
Katie Wadsworth (8)   10
Francesca Hipperson (9)   10
Hannah Braithwaite (10)   11
Zoe Meek (8)   11
Callum Kenny (9)   12
Amelia Briggs (8)   13
Catherine Smith (9)   13
Sam Morton (11)   14
Zoe Cuckow (9)   14
Chanelle Smith (8)   15
George Alexander Grange (8)   15
Chris Lyons (9)   16
Ryan Cornelissen & Stuart Duffy (8)   16
Corrin Hudson (8)   17
Rebecca Heeley (9)   17
Jack Farrar (10)   18
Anna Cuckow (9)   19

Amy Sparling (8)   19
Kerry Waite (8)   20
Krystina Mawer (9)   20
Thomas Goldie & Jack Farrar (11)   21

England Lane JI School
Scott Temple (10)   22
Zeta Livsey (10)   22
Robert Stephenson (10)   23
Charlotte Hopps (11)   24
Susanna Atkinson (9)   25

Glusburn CP School
Amelia Hopkinson & Zoe Robinson (8)   25
Sally Cheung (8)   26
John Varley (8)   26
Jessica Sadler (8)   26
Daniele Santabarbara (8)   27
Daniel Dejong (7)   27
Joshua Tones (8)   27
Matthew Taylor (8)   28
Eleanor O'Driscoll (8)   28
Katie Stoney (8)   28
Sam Johnson (8)   29
Adam Birch (8)   29
Hannah Cairns (8)   29

Horbury Bridge CE JI Primary School
Amelia Dale (10)   30
Lauren Hammill (8)   30
Nikki Lonsdale (8)   31
Elliot Milnes (8)   32
George Dale (9)   33
Lucy Denton (8)   34
Paige Mitchell (8)   35
Charlotte Rawden (9)   35
Bradley Gearey (9)   36
Damian Brayshaw (10)   36

Thomas Leyshon (9)   36
Kirsty Robinson (8)   37
Ryan Verity (9)   38
Laura Madden (9)   38
Jamie Lamont (10)   39
Eleanor Mitchell (9)   39
Emily Schofield (10)   40
Aletia Harper (9)   40
Hannah Denton (9)   41
Rachel Walls (10)   41
Amy Cudworth (10)   42
Herbie Naylor-Mayers (10)   42

Inglebrook School
Cheyenne Grainger (9)   43
Laura Pindar (9)   43
Jenny Barker (9)   44
Charlotte Bennett (9)   45
Alice Sandham (9)   45
Olivia Shelton (10)   46
Sophie Astle (10)   46
Ashley Elliott (9)   47
Naomi Knaggs (10)   47
Rachel Cook (9)   48
Hadley Stringer (10)   49
Andrew Earnshaw (9)   50
Christopher Speight (10)   50
Thomas Hicks (9)   51

Larks Hill JI School
Edward Grayson (8)   51
Emily Carr (8)   52
Matthew Holmes (9)   52
Hannah Young (9)   53
Bradley Wilson (9)   53
Max Pepper (9)   54
Helena Wood (9)   54
Matthew Riley (9)   55

Liam Threlfall (9)	55
Andrew Parry (8)	56
Sophie Lambert (8)	56
Joshua Atkinson (9)	57
Joshua Metcalfe (9)	57
Madeleine Prew (8)	58
Elizabeth Haddington (8)	58
Christopher Harris (9)	59
Kalon Everitt (9)	59
Rosanna Loftus (8)	60
Chloe Mylonas (8)	60
Heather Lindsay (8)	61
Ben Chappell (8)	62
Alicia Lemm	62
Jessica Adlington (9)	62
Matthew Lindsay (8)	63
Christopher Walker (9)	63
Ryan James Langley (8)	64
Sarah Vause (9)	64
Lana Hopkins (9)	65
Georgina Myers (8)	65
Christopher Gill (8)	66

Malsis School

Peter Green (10)	66
William Leigh-Bramwell (9)	67
Antonia Benson (11)	67
Charlotte Warburton (11)	68
Jonathan Hutchinson (10)	68
Xavier Greenwood (8)	69
Sophie McMullan (9)	69
Jessica Bailey (11)	70
Todd Robinson (10)	70
Harry Warburton (9)	71
Charles Farnes (9)	71
Jonathan Wells (9)	72
Nicole Dadhley (9)	72
Edward Smith (9)	73

Henry Brook (11)   73
Nicholas Thompson (9)   74
Joshua Greenwood (11)   75
James Healey (9)   75
Bryony Harrap (11)   76
Jennifer Slack (9)   76
Freddy Hammond (11)   77
Elliott Bell (9)   77
Sarah Naylor (11)   78
Andrew Denman (11)   78
Vanessa Bailey (9)   79
Jacey Rawsthorne (9)   79
Jack Starr (11)   79
Rabia Qureshi (10)   80
Christopher Gliniecki (10)   80
Charlie Pilkington (9)   81
Ramit Abrol (11)   81
Charles Naylor (10)   82
Anthony Ingham (10)   82
Alex Ickringill (10)   83
Joseph Webster (11)   83
Ollie Greenwood (10)   84
Todd Robinson (10)   84

Mill Dam JI School

Alexandra Bacon (10)   85
Nathan Morgan (9)   86
Alaina Everson (8)   86
Oliver Hemingway Brooke (8)   87
Chris Paterson (8)   87
Samantha Taylor (9)   88
Francesca Ellis (11)   88

North Featherstone JI School

Summer Lea Bedford (8)   89
Chantel Adamson (10)   89
Bradley Wood (9)   90
Daniel Parker (8)   90

Ashleigh Olivia Davies (9)	91
Thomas Garland-Jones (9)	92
Ellie Nicholson (8)	93
James Browne (9)	93
Paige Leach (9)	94
David Blackburn (8)	94
Alex Guy (8)	95
Laura Hunter (9)	95
Coral Midgley (8)	96
Adam Short (11)	96
Jessica Seaman (7)	97
Tiffany Bland (11)	97
Donna Marie Connelly (8)	98
Jade Guest (10)	99
Jo-Louise Knibb (11)	100
Amy Windmill (10)	101
Bethany Hiorns (11)	102
Jack Nicholson (8)	102
Danielle Gale (11)	103
Louise Garland-Jones (10)	104
Abby Leach (11)	105
Sean Stones (11)	105
Amy Schofield (10)	106
Nichola Howarth (9)	107

Oyster Park Junior School

Samuel Ian Parkinson (11)	107
Bradley Thornton (9)	108
Chloe Beattie (10)	108
Marcus Dale (10)	109
Ashleigh Carr (9)	109
Shanelle Bateman (10)	109
Zarina Earnshaw (9)	110
Karin Ward (10)	110
Jordan Palmer (10)	110
Daniel Carter (10)	111
Jaime Blythe (11)	111
Terri-Leigh Woolford (11)	111

Jade Blackburn (11)   112
Alice Carlyle (10)   112
Leanne Kirby (11)   113
Reanna Wallis (10)   113
Demi Davies (8)   114
Jessica Strong (11)   114
Ella Louise Spence (8)   115
Mandy Louise Armstrong (9)   116
Zoe Brain (9)   116
Daniel Swift (9)   117
Megan Noone (9)   117
Becky Hand (9)   118
Jade Barker (8)   118
Kirsty Guthrie (9)   119
Josh Birdsall (9)   119
Bethany Field (8)   120
Ashley Yorke (8)   120
Chelsea Jaine Land (11)   121
Ryan Smith (11)   121
Aran Starbuck (10)   122
Jessica Taylor (10)   122
Ryan Randle (10)   123
Adam Rothwell (10)   123
Hayley Harling (10)   124
Daniel Moore (11)   124
Kiera Whitworth (11)   125
Theresa Begley (11)   126

Ripponden JI School

Hanley Gaynor (7)   126
Jonathan Porritt (8)   126
Isobel Wimbleton (7)   127
Toby Rogers (7)   127
Rebecca Callister (8)   128
Ashley Campbell (8)   128
Charlotte Wolstenholme (7)   129
Meganne Green (8)   129
Jorja Nuttall (8)   130

Connor Stephenson (7)   130
Scott Sutcliffe (7)   131
Perry Stephen (8)   131

St Andrew's Junior School, Brighouse

Jack Johnstone (9)   132
Eva Khan (10)   133
Gareth Hopkins (9)   133
Chloe Kitcher (10)   134
Emily Johnson (9)   135
Sarah Drake (10)   135
Annabel Wilson (9)   136
Amelia Thurlow (9)   137
Elise Marsden (9)   138
Stephen Hughes (9)   139
Georgina Graham (9)   140
Lauren O'Brien (10)   141
Rachel Hunt (10)   142
Emily Beth Parkinson (9)   143
Faith Thewlis (10)   143
Natasha Smith (10)   144
Rebecca Howard (9)   144

St Clare's RC Primary School, Bradford

Gemma Melhuish (10)   145
Lauren Hickey (8)   145
Gabrielle Crabtree (10)   146
Mary-Clare Newsham (10)   147
Jane Nicholson (10)   147
Alice Jukes (10)   148
Daniel Parkinson (9)   148
Emma Croot (11)   149
Thomas Lock (9)   150
Eleanor Willis (11)   151

St Hilda's School, Wakefield

Catherine Mitchell (7)   152
Jodie Burnley (8)   153

Emily Lodge (7)   153
Eleanor Newton (8)   154
Amber Johnson (8)   154
Harriet Willings (8)   155
Rhea Patel (8)   156
Sehrish Butt (8)   157
Melissa Doyles (8)   157
Chloe Sunderland (7)   158
Holli Yu (7)   159
Jade Wolfenden (8)   159
Hayleigh Edson (8)   160
Natalie English (8)   161
Bethany Johnson (9)   162

St Mary's CE Primary School, Boston Spa
Emma Grainger (10)   162
Grace Barrett (8)   163
Naomi Barrow (8)   163
Liam Livesley (8)   164
Polly Whitelam (8)   164
Laura Pattison (9)   165
Jessica Coates (9)   166
Natalie Heaton (9)   167
Naomi Allan (10)   167
Holly Bonelle (10)   168

St Matthew's RC Primary School, Bradford
Grace Lindsey (9)   169
Kieran Lad (10)   169
Sophie Priestley (10)   170
Rebecca Wilson (11)   171
Dean Armitage (11)   171
Bethany Taylor (11)   172
Riccardo Coppola (11)   172
Alex Conlon (9)   173
Thomas Stokes (10)   174

Sacred Heart Primary School, Ilkley

Morag Gillon (9)	175
Andrew Ettenfield (8)	176
Jade Davy (8)	177
Ruth Doherty (8)	178
Helena Below (9)	179
Michael Loy (9)	180
Natasha Verspyck (8)	181

Sacred Heart RC Primary School, Sowerby Bridge

Kara Parry (10)	181
Sarah Cahill	182
Callum Rimmer (9)	182
Daniel Ball (9)	183
Charlie Wilkinson (10)	183
Amber Ransley (10)	184
Matthew Carey (10)	185
Rebecca Kenyon (10)	185
Sean Regan (10)	186
Max Brown (9)	186
Ryan Murphy (10)	187
David Carter (10)	187
Shannon Horridge (9)	188
Colin Millns (10)	188
Bethany Leslie (9)	189
Alex Rhodes (9)	189
Ellie Gerrard (10)	190
Amy Leonard (9)	190
Bethany Horner (9)	191
Darrell Bingham (9)	192
Kerry Lister (9)	192
Lili Cordingley (8)	193
Nathaniel Powell (8)	193
Lucy Mitchell (8)	194

Sutton CP School

Kane Booker (10)	194
Thomas Ogden (11)	195

Robert Berry (11)	195
Samantha Harrison (10)	196
Abigail Lorimer (10)	196
Chris Raine (10)	197
Simon Hargraves (10)	197
Thomas Wood (11)	197
Katy Stares (10)	198
Emma Greenwood (10)	198
Joseph Robertshaw (11)	199
Daniel Wild (11)	199
James Smith (11)	200
Daniel Hart (11)	200
Katie Booker (11)	201
Daniel Longbottom (11)	201
Jack Barraclough (11)	202
Isobel Sutcliffe (10)	202
Matthew Burton (10)	203
Sarah Liu (11)	203
Lottie Hicks (10)	204
Chris Riley (11)	204
Sam Harrison (10)	205
Charlotte McPike (10)	205
Findley Harrison (11)	206
Lynsey Vincent (11)	206
Bethany Ellison (10)	207

Upper Whitley JI School

Christina Foster (11)	207
Daniel Archer (10)	207
James Clarkson (9)	208
Thomas Sowerby (9)	208
Rachel Adams (10)	208
Jamie Holmes (10)	209
Emily Stalmach (8)	209
Dale Jones (9)	210
Lisa Bentley (9)	210
Whitney-Jayne Boswell (9)	210
Luke Archer (8)	211

Megan McKay (10)   211
Katie Wilson (8)   212
Naomi Bamforth (8)   212

Wellington Primary School
Jodie Cork-Dove (9)   213
Chloe Sutcliffe (11)   214
Jessica Fisher (9)   215
Andrew Shanley (9)   216
Bradley Marsden (8)   217
Sarah Davidson (8)   218
Lewis Ragan (9)   219
James Emmett (9)   220
Abigail Hirst (9)   221
Sam McMahon (9)   222
James Archer (9)   223

Westville House School
Joel Harrison (9)   223
Jennifer Caisley (8)   224
Jessica Peppiate (9)   225
Daniel Jeffrey (9)   226
Sophie Patchett (8)   226
Lydia Holloway (8)   227
James Smith (9)   228
Chloe Moss (8)   229
Alexander Rose (8)   230
Edward Hardy (8)   230
William Shelton (9)   231
Jonathan McGurk (9)   232
Philip Hydleman (8)   232
Roselle Hirst (9)   233

The Poems

FOOTBALL

He tackled
He passed
He shot
And scored
He whirled
And twirled
And made them dizzy

He jumped
He ran
He flew
He crashed . . .
And broke the bar!

Joseph Lawton (10)

MISS SCANLON

She's a cheerful, shiny chair.
She's a friendly bear.
She's a car racing everywhere.
She's a young bird singing sweetly.
She's a bright summer's day.
She's a smell of a poppy.
She's a rosy red rose.
She's a shiny, yellow rose.

Marya Hussain (9)

FIRST DAY AT SCHOOL

On the first day of school
It was good.
But then I spilt my pop, on my top
I was mad
And I got sad.
I cried
And then it dried.
On the second day of school Mrs Bush
Said, 'Come on, rush.'
I had a best friend called Sarah,
We played together,
We played on the bikes together,
We painted together
And that was my friend Sarah for you.
I got done,
It was not fun.

Natalie Hirst (9)

SADNESS

Sadness is when you cry,
You get very shy and lie,
Then you feel very lonely,
Very quiet and talk slowly.

Gemma Pearce (9)

OUR WORLD

They are brutally beating the trees,
Chopping them down,
Slicing their roots,
Raking them up,
But why? Why?
What will be left?
A flat, a road,
Not a bush or a tree,
Just a concrete world.
No trees for nests,
No grubs for worms,
No greenery,
Just concrete,
This is your next generation's world.

Joshua Vickers (11)
Christ Church (VA) Junior School

OUR WORLD

Destroying the Earth to make way for cars,
Animals' habitats giving way to tar.
Concrete instead of greens and trees,
What happened to autumn's golden brown leaves?
The colours of beautiful summer flowers,
We've wiped away all of these things.
It's so awful what man-made brings,
Do you want your children to see only grey and black?
Oil in seas and leaves on the ground,
All we had was ours to share,
But people have used it like a dirty palette
And washed away all God's colours.

Katie Whitehead (11)
Christ Church (VA) Junior School

OUR WORLD

Think of a grey dull world;
Your child growing up not knowing about flowers and trees.
A gift given once,
For all eternity.
The old world destroyed,
Replaced with a new world.
The sky the last colour,
Soon will die out.
Save the valleys! Save the hills!
Save the last petal that falls!
The green grass is being torn away,
The habitats have disappeared.
The new world has woken,
The litter monster is walking,
The bulldozer is rolling,
Nature is dying,
Concrete in its place,
You have made our new world.

Lisa Doyle (11)
Christ Church (VA) Junior School

OUR WORLD

A beautiful world of nature,
Flowers, trees and animals,
Gone with one bulldozer,
Replaced with dull concrete.

Children will be colourblind
And not know what a flower is,
The world around them colourful
Or grey? It's up to you!

So please, think what you're doing,
The Earth's hanging on for its life,
Don't kill it because
It will be gone forever.

The Earth's an ashtray,
A big dump or skip,
A land full of chewing gum,
A street full of rubbish.

The world was once green,
With a light blue sky,
But now it's grey,
Just ask yourself why?

The flower's a creature
That lives in our heart,
So please leave it living,
Don't pull it apart.

Just think for a minute,
What would the world be
Without flowers in the ground
And fish in the sea?

Charlotte Balmforth (11)
Christ Church (VA) Junior School

OUR WORLD

Torturing land for profit,
Tearing away Earth's skin,
No living plants,
A dull colourless place.
No life for poultry,
Innocent in prison.
A concrete world,
Trees and plants
Are badly killed,
While towns and cities,
Forever get larger.
Is this how you want it?
Didn't think so.
Do your part,
Don't drop litter,
Look after our world.

Shane Dow (11)
Christ Church (VA) Junior School

OUR WORLD

The land is dying because of you.
Here is a world given to us,
Destroy it, kill it! Why?
Eating the world with big yellow machines,
Why do you demolish a living thing?
Over the hills and far away, is now past the dirty factories.
What do you say?
Red and yellow, green and blue
Has changed to grey, grey and grey.
This is because of what you do!
Life is new every second of the day,
Keep some flowers and chickens to lay,
Day after day a tree dies,
Bye bye tree,
Bye bye lives.

Sophie Whitehead (11)
Christ Church (VA) Junior School

WHAT AM I?

I am a . . .
    Cage climber,
    Deep sleeper,
    Loud nibbler,
    Cheese eater,
    Water licker,
    Food gobbler,
    Fast runner,
    Cage rattler
    And a bed lover!

Hamster.

Natalie Mawer (9)
Collingham Lady Hastings CE Primary School

WHEN WE'RE ON VENUS

Have you seen us
When we're on Venus
Waving our arms about?
When we go there
There isn't much air
And so we're not able to shout

It's ever so hot
So we sweat quite a lot
The air is just acid and dust
And what a palaver!
There's all of this lava
From when the volcanoes went bust

We can't see you
Cos the clouds spoil the view
But with a telescope you may have seen us
We're on one of the stars
Quite close to Mars
What a wonderful visit to Venus!

Lizzy Quirke (10)
Collingham Lady Hastings CE Primary School

LEFT OUT

I was crying all day
I felt like a droopy flower
My legs were like ice
And I was furious with my friend
My arms were like rocks
She took no notice of me
She turned her back.

Katherine Duncan (8)
Collingham Lady Hastings CE Primary School

OUR TEACHER

Our teacher in our class is bound to weigh 12 stone-one,
She hides in the cupboard
And we saw her eat a chocolate bun!

She has skinny little fingers and skinny little toes,
She wears ugly green skirts
And she picks her nose!

She's very short and very fat,
She's petty in every way,
She wears a stupid floral hat.

Our teacher is not a pretty sight,
As she hits you with a stripy cane
And she's in your dreams at night!

Kizzy Strodder (9)
Collingham Lady Hastings CE Primary School

NEPTUNE

N ight-time is here, I look up to the sky
E ndless darkness, I'm wondering why . . .
P lanets and stars are up there somewhere
T rying to see them, I don't think they're there
U p in the sky, I look to the stars
N obody knows if there's anyone on Mars
E ndless, endless, endless . . .

Space!

Caroline Simpson (10)
Collingham Lady Hastings CE Primary School

I WISH THAT . . .

I wish that the flowers would always blossom
So the world would be filled with colour.

I wish that the birds would always chirp their merry tunes
High above the trees.

I wish dogs would bark happily, cats would purr proudly
As they play together.

I wish that monkeys would never be harmed
By the land grabbers.

I wish that the fish would swim playfully
In the silky blue sea.

I wish that the world would always be beautiful
For you and me.

Katie Wadsworth (8)
Collingham Lady Hastings CE Primary School

A PLACE WHERE NO ONE'S BEEN

A place where no one's been might have lots of trees,
A place where no one's been might be very green.
A place where no one's been might just be plain blue,
A place where no one's been might be made from glue!
It's all very well, this place where no one's been,
But the place that I know I've been to is Dream Land.

Francesca Hipperson (9)
Collingham Lady Hastings CE Primary School

SEA CREATURES

Jellyfish, jellyfish, wriggle around,
They sting people when they are found,
Whales, whales, sprout up water,
When they are babies they are a lot shorter,
Sharks, sharks, love to eat meat,
Especially their favourite meat - feet.
Eels, eels, are like lightning
And they are frightening.
Starfish, starfish, are so, so spotty,
But they can get really knotty.
Fishes, fishes, swim with grace,
But some of the fish swim in a race.
Swimming around, not making a sound,
Sea creatures abound!

Hannah Braithwaite (10)
Collingham Lady Hastings CE Primary School

THE FAMILY DINING ROOM

In the dining room we eat our food,
My brother gets in a mood.

We pick up our knife and fork,
My mum starts to talk.

I stab my meat,
My nan starts to eat.

We're coming to the end of our feast,
My dad looks like a great big beast

And as for me . . .
I've finished my tea.

Zoe Meek (8)
Collingham Lady Hastings CE Primary School

THE SALOOO

I shout, I scream, I scare people too, when they're in the loo,
I am the Salooo!
They think I'm the toilet drain flushing away until . . .
They see me.
I am blue and green and pink, with a golden tongue
And razor-sharp teeth
To chew the girl who ventures into the toilet.
I am the monster that hides in the loo
I am the Salooo!
My friends say I'm hideous, I say thank you,
I am the monster that hides in the loo.
I have a face that broke 1000 mirrors (it's a world record you know!)
I have evil eyes and a wicked grin,
I even make the teachers scream when they enter the loo!
I am the Salooo!
I am 8 feet tall and can't really fit in the loo,
But I squeeze myself small and manage to.
I am the Salooo!
I watch for humans approaching and then . . .
I have no ears but a bloodthirsty mouth.
I have one thick eyebrow to tell everyone I mean business
(Because I do!)
I am the Salooo!
I have 4 huge arms and a long slimy tail
With a bird's talon on my single leg!
I think I came from the sea originally but I don't know,
I admit I'm a bit thick, I do,
I know who I am though,
I am the Salooo!

Callum Kenny (9)
Collingham Lady Hastings CE Primary School

THE POND

Sitting by the pond, my back is warmed by the sun,
Gazing into the waters I see a tiny water world,
A silver water beetle standing firm in his shining metal armour,
Guards the entrance to the little shimmering world,
The stones at the side of the pond are his Ben Nevis
                                        and Mount Everest.
Graceful pond skaters like birds of the air,
Weaving in and out of the pondweed trees,
I wish I was light then I could walk on water,
Suddenly a sparkling stickleback zooms past my eyes,
A silver streak of lightning,
He hovers over a black cloud of tadpoles,
At once the black swarm rises up into the water,
Twirling, twisting, like a mass of little kites.
A sinister water spider underneath the lily pad,
Tries to hide and slinks away into his bubble chamber,
I thought the pond was a peaceful place,
But it is full of danger,
I am glad I am sitting safe, warmed by the sun.

Amelia Briggs (8)
Collingham Lady Hastings CE Primary School

THE CAT

See the sleek black fur,
Watch her as she purrs,
See and watch her beady eyes,
In the dark and midnight skies,
Watch her as she climbs so high,
A few minutes later,
She's touching the sky.

Catherine Smith (9)
Collingham Lady Hastings CE Primary School

THE WATER CYCLE POEM

I am the sun all gleaming and hot
There is the water I need to pick up
I shine all day until it gets late
Waiting for the water to evaporate

Then it rises into the sky
To make a wet cloud way up high
The clouds get dark and bulge under strain
They *explode* their load and scatter with rain

With the grey cloud disappearing
The bright yellow sun can be seen again
Ready to make raindrops
To bring life to Earth once again.

Sam Morton (11)
Collingham Lady Hastings CE Primary School

THE ANNOYING TWIN

The annoying twin,
Will always be there.
Funny, chatty, strange,
Like a good shadow,
Like a voice I can't get rid of.
She makes me feel glad,
But still no one notices me,
At least I've always got somebody to play with.

Zoe Cuckow (9)
Collingham Lady Hastings CE Primary School

MY DOG

My dog is very furry,
My dog is very kind,
My dog is very sweet
And she is all mine.

My dog can be clever,
My dog can be smart,
My dog can be nosy
And my dog can take part.

My dog is very friendly,
My dog is very loveable,
My dog is very funny
And my dog can make you laugh.

My dog is white,
My dog glows at night,
My dog has big brown eyes
That shine in the moonlight.

Chanelle Smith (8)
Collingham Lady Hastings CE Primary School

ANGRY WORDS

Angry words are like
Electricity running down my spine,
Swords digging into me,
People drowning
And all these things are bad.

George Alexander Grange (8)
Collingham Lady Hastings CE Primary School

THE MAGIC CHAIN

Greek soldiers were in battle
Fighting Trojans who were slaughtered
Wearing armour held by chains
Striding on the watered plains

A Trojan sword broke the chain
Which dropped upon a horse's mane
Hittite ties it on the reins
Then pulls the loop to halt the colt.

Chris Lyons (9)
Collingham Lady Hastings CE Primary School

YOU HAVE . . .

You have eyes like footballs.
You have a nose like a mountain.
You have teeth like slabs of ice.
You have hair like a fountain.
You have a body like a tower.
You have arms like giant branches.
You have ears like enormous flowers.
You have legs like huge tree trunks.
You have amazing power.

You are a giant.

Ryan Cornelissen & Stuart Duffy (8)
Collingham Lady Hastings CE Primary School

MY CAT, NINJA

My cat is ginger
And I call him Ninja,
I know when he's proud,
Because he purrs out loud,
He's the cutest I know
And I love him so,
He has a bright silver collar,
Which cost more than a dollar,
A bell that rings and goes
Ding-aling-aling.

Corrin Hudson (8)
Collingham Lady Hastings CE Primary School

PLANETS

Dazzling and dancing alone in space
Orbiting the sun, in an endless race
Twisting and turning amongst the stars
Planets of mystery, from Saturn to Mars
The planets are very, very old
Some are very, very cold
All the planets are the shape of a ball
And some planets are quite small.

Rebecca Heeley (9)
Collingham Lady Hastings CE Primary School

SOMEBODY

Somebody is going to show me . . .
A unicorn,
A dragon
And a Hydra,
With its poisonous fangs,
For I have never seen them before.

Somebody is going to show me . . .
The planets Urachus and Fallachus,
The stars and their burning cores,
Beyond the universe
And far, far away,
For I have never been there before.

Somebody is going to show me . . .
Each layer of the Earth,
The deepest of oceans
And the highest of mountains,
Which have never been discovered,
For I have never reached there before.

Somebody is going to show me . . .
The god of wind,
The saviour of flowers,
The heart of rain
And the soul of heat,
For I have never seen them before.

This person to me,
Has red silk robes,
Shining white hair,
Twinkling eyes
And the kindest of hands,
Which lead me.

This person is God.

Jack Farrar (10)
Collingham Lady Hastings CE Primary School

THERE I WAS SWIMMING ALONG

I am swimming along
Doing not a thing at all,
When down came a maggot,
Just like a ball.

So I gobbled it down,
Oh look, there is a hook,
Then my face made a frown.

So I get pulled up by the hook
And around I look
And what I see is a fisherman,
Reading a book.

'Oh, he's not big,
Better throw him back.'
I make a splash, so put on your mac,
'Throw him back,'
I'm free!

Anna Cuckow (9)
Collingham Lady Hastings CE Primary School

AUTUMN

Berries fall day and night,
Colours are so very bright,
The juices are a pure delight,
The robins appear in the twinkling moonlight

Leaves fall off lovely trees,
That's the sign of the autumn breeze,
You walk through the crunchy leaves,
Shivering in the autumn freeze.

Amy Sparling (8)
Collingham Lady Hastings CE Primary School

GOD'S GIFTS

Ziggy-zaggy zebra
Cuddly, cute cat
Playful puppy
Beautiful bat

Big brown bear
Wonderful whale
Prancing pony
Slimy snail

Porky pigs
Cheeky chimps
All these animals
Are God's gifts.

Kerry Waite (8)
Collingham Lady Hastings CE Primary School

WIBBLE AND WOBBLE

Wibble and wobble
Oh did they squabble,
All day and all night
It gave me a fright.
The walls would crumble
Which made my legs tumble,
The tables would break
And I would shake.
The chairs would rattle
That would annoy the cattle,
What silly penguins they were!

Krystina Mawer (9)
Collingham Lady Hastings CE Primary School

THE TAP WATER RAP

There was a drop of water,
Who fell down from the sky.
He fell into a river,
I swear, it's not a lie.

He got as far as Scarborough,
But his journey hadn't ended,
He was sucked up once again,
He knew it was intended.

He rose into a big black cloud,
Along with all the others.
He wondered what would happen next,
To him and all his brothers.

'We're getting really heavy man,'
Said Bob, the biggest drip.
'It won't be very long now,
Before we all jump ship.'

'We'll trickle down the mountainside
And collar that young fella,
Let's see how long it takes before
He puts up his umbrella.'

Thomas Goldie & Jack Farrar (11)
Collingham Lady Hastings CE Primary School

THE BEACH

I was on the beach in the winter,
A plank of wood gave me a splinter,
The gritty sand,
Hurt my hand,
The sea was rough,
That's it, I have had enough.

On the beach in the sun,
A sandcastle I made was nearly done,
With a bucket and spade,
A hole we made,
Was flooded by water.

Scott Temple (10)
England Lane JI School

WHY DID YOU GO?

So many things have happened
We wanted you to share
So many times we've needed you
And wished that you were there
We think about you always
And talk about you too
We have so many memories
But wished we still had you.

Zeta Livsey (10)
England Lane JI School

OUR WORLD

The world is a beautiful place,
It's fit for the human race,
But if people pollute it,
It will dilute it
And people will think it's a big disgrace.

People say animals are bad,
But it's them who's going mad,
If they weren't there,
We wouldn't share,
The joy it brings today.

That's why we must respect our world,
Be grateful for what we've got,
Some people have nothing,
Some people are rich,
It's easy to tell which is which.

I'm bringing my poem to an end,
Hoping a message has gone out to the people who spend,
Be grateful for what you've got,
Because others haven't a lot.

Robert Stephenson (10)
England Lane JI School

THE FIRST DAY OF SPRING

On the first day of spring,
The birds would always sing,
I always loved to see,
How careful they would be.

A flower blooming every day
And I would always say,
'How pretty do they look?
They're better than a book.'

The birds lay their eggs
And out pops a head,
A little bird is laid,
Every single day!

The kittens jump and play
And then they run away,
They play with butterflies
And their mums say that's not wise.

The children play out till late,
Way past eight,
The light nights are here,
There's nothing to fear.

It's getting hotter as they play
And then they look at each other and say,
'Let's go home, it's time for bed,
I want to get in my nest!'
Easter is near,
The bunny's coming here,
We'll wake up tomorrow with chocolate to eat,
Everyone's coming out to have a big feast!

Exciting spring is coming to an end,
I hope you found a great new friend!

Charlotte Hopps (11)
England Lane JI School

THE WORLD OF MAGIC

Books of enchantments,
Witches and wands,
Wizards and potions,
Frogs from the ponds.

Old books of spells,
Tall, pointy hats,
Abracadabra,
Witches' black cats.

Brown, wooden broomsticks,
Witches take flight,
Crossing the full moon,
At dead of night.

Two kinds of magic,
Two trails to track,
Good versus evil,
White versus black.

Susanna Atkinson (9)
England Lane JI School

WHITE

White is snow, cold and wet.
White is the full moon up in the starry sky.
White is the sky when it's full of fluffy clouds.
White is a blank piece of paper before we write on it.
White is a soft feather pillow that I sleep on at night.
White is the whiteboard that we read each day in school,
That tells us to write a poem for you.

Amelia Hopkinson & Zoe Robinson (8)
Glusburn CP School

SUMMER

Summer is gardens filled with colourful flowers.
Summer is people wearing fluffy towels.
Summer is when there is hot weather.
Summer is people wearing jackets that are leather.
Summer is when you splash in the pool,
Of course you go in to help you to cool.
Summer is when baby animals come out.
Summer is when outside, we all run about
And that's the poem of summer and fun
Because I'm always glad to be back in the sun.

Sally Cheung (8)
Glusburn CP School

CHRISTMAS

Christmas is the wonderful excitement of presents.
Christmas is eating delicious dinner.
Christmas is to go sledging on snow up on the hill.
Christmas is lights that look like colourful stars.

John Varley (8)
Glusburn CP School

WINTER

Winter is feeling as cold as ice
Winter is drinking chocolate whilst watching children play in the snow
Winter is snuggling up warm in bed
Winter is Christmas and feeling excited
Winter is snow covering the ground like a blanket.

Jessica Sadler (8)
Glusburn CP School

RED

Red is burning ashes on a bonfire.
Red is tongues licking lovely apple sour lollies.
Red is a Ferrari, zooming by, fast.
Red is blood running through your veins.

Daniele Santabarbara (8)
Glusburn CP School

WINTER

Winter is for sledging in the crisp white snow.
Winter is for sliding on the smooth dark ice.
Winter is for making ghostly angels in the snow.
Winter is for building large fat snowmen.
Winter is for making footprints in the snow.

Daniel Dejong (7)
Glusburn CP School

CHRISTMAS

Christmas is the excitement of new presents that Santa brings for us.
Christmas is going sledging up at Devil's Drop on the crisp white snow.
Christmas is the lovely, delicious dinner my mum cooks for us.
Christmas is the sparkling lights glittering on the Christmas tree.

Joshua Tones (8)
Glusburn CP School

RED

Red is burning ashes in the fire.
Red is a tomato round like a ball.
Red is lips when my mum wears lipstick.
Red is a Ferrari travelling as fast as a bullet.
Red is a very red apple.

Matthew Taylor (8)
Glusburn CP School

RED

Red is blood inside your body.
Red is a tomato as round as a ball.
Red is lips on a hot summer's day.
Red is sweet strawberry jam in a sandwich.
Red is a telephone box to ring for help.
Red is a juicy apple picked fresh from a tree.

Eleanor O'Driscoll (8)
Glusburn CP School

RED IS . . .

Red is blood inside your body.
Red is a tomato as round as a ball.
Red is lips on a hot summer's day.
Red is strawberry jam in a sandwich.
Red is a telephone box to make calls.
Red is a juicy apple, picked fresh from a tree.
Red is a postbox to post your letters.

Katie Stoney (8)
Glusburn CP School

GREEN

Green is slimy snot from your nose.
Green is a long, winding garden hose.
Green is the new-mown grass in a summer garden.
Green is a very seasick passenger in a boat.
Green is the mould on a piece of old bread.
Green is the sporty shoes worn by a sport star.
Green is the new chairs in Class 8.
Green is a cool hairdo worn by an idiot!

Sam Johnson (8)
Glusburn CP School

HAPPINESS

Happiness is Christmas and finding lots of presents.
Happiness is going home from school on Friday night.
Happiness is going to the toy shop to buy a new toy.
Happiness is going on holiday on a sunny day.
Happiness is receiving lots of chocolate Easter eggs.
Happiness is learning to ride my shiny new bike.

Adam Birch (8)
Glusburn CP School

BLUE IS . . .

Blue is a blueberry picked fresh from a bush.
Blue is the waves of the deep dark sea.
Blue is cold lips on a winter's day.
Blue is the light of the summer sky.
Blue is when someone you love has died.
Blue is the fifth colour of the rainbow.

Hannah Cairns (8)
Glusburn CP School

MONSTERS

Creeping round the bedroom
Hiding under the bed
Some suck out your insides
Some bite off your head
Some are great big viruses
Some are flesh and blood
All of them are evil
But none of them are good
Some have razor claws
That swipe you clean in two
Some have gigantic jaws
Stronger than ten of you
So if you have a monster
Don't just lose your head
Just do the simplest thing
Let him eat you instead.

Amelia Dale (10)
Horbury Bridge CE JI Primary School

THE SEA

The sea is crashing.
The sea is rough.
The sea is bashing.
The sea is tough.
The sea is like lightning.
The sea is frightening.
The sea throws itself to the rocks.

Lauren Hammill (8)
Horbury Bridge CE JI Primary School

ANIMAL ALPHABET

A lligators snap at you.
B ees buzz at you.
C rocodiles scare you.
D ucks quack at you.
E lephants spray water at you.
F ish bubble and gurgle at you.
G orillas growl at you.
H ungry hippos yawn at you.
I nsects *hummmmm* . . . at you.
J aguars try to bite you.
K angaroos bounce up to you.
L ions roar at you.
M ad monkeys climb around you.
N ightingales squawk at you.
O striches are bigger than you.
P enguins waddle up to you.
Q uails fly above you.
R obins chirp at you.
S loths hang above you.
T urtles swim slowly up to you.
U nicorns puzzle you.
V ipers hiss and spit at you.
W hales come up to breathe water at you.
X . . . this animal's a secret *shhhh!*
Y aks moo at you.
Z ookeepers watch you.

Nikki Lonsdale (8)
Horbury Bridge CE JI Primary School

ANIMAL ALPHABET

A lligators snap at you
B aboons throw bananas at you
C obras stare at you
D olphins swim towards you
E lephants blow water at you
F ish swim towards you
G uinea pigs store food for you
H ippos yawn at you
I guanas lay eggs for you
J aguars climb for you
K oala bears stare at you
L arge lions roar at you
M arsupials carry their young
N ew newts hatch
O ctopi hide from you
P arrots squawk at you
Q uails fly at you
R abbits hop to you
S nakes slither to you
T arantulas try to blind you
U nicorns look weird for you
V enomous frogs jump at you
W ater buffalos charge at you
X . . . this name is a secret
Y aks moo at you
Z ebras run away from you.

Elliot Milnes (8)
Horbury Bridge CE JI Primary School

ANIMAL ALPHABET

A lligators snap at you
B aboons ooh at you
C ats miaow at you
D ogs bark at you
E lephants squirt water at you
F ish scatter from you
G orillas pound their chests at you
H ippos splash at you
I nsects sting you
J aguars run away from you
K angaroos bounce on you
L ions grrr at you
M onkeys pick your hair
N ewts wriggle away from you
O ctopi splash at you
P arrots squawk at you
Q uails flap at you
R ats scatter from you
S nakes show their fangs to you
T arantulas creep up on you
U nicorns puzzle you
V enomous snakes hiss at you
W hales swim away from you
X ... (This name is a secret)
Y aks moo at you
Z ookeepers watch you.

George Dale (9)
Horbury Bridge CE JI Primary School

ANIMAL ALPHABET

A   lligators snap and stare at you.
B   ears growl and glare at you.
C   ats claw and miaow at you.
D   ingos bark and scare you.
E   lephants squirt water and stomp at you.
F   ish bubble and gurgle at you.
G   orillas roar at you.
H   ungry hippos yawn and ignore you.
I   nsects fly away from you.
J   aguars bite and growl at you.
K   angaroos jump high over you.
L   lamas bite and spit at you.
M   ad monkeys laugh and giggle at you.
N   ewts wriggle and splash at you.
O   striches run fast and lay eggs for you.
P   enguins waddle up to you.
Q   uails squeak and chirp at you.
R   abbits jump away from you.
S   loths hang upside down and look at you.
T   ortoise walk very slowly to you.
U   nicorns don't exist for you.
V   enomous snakes hiss at you.
W   hales open their mouth and swallow you.
X   . . . this creature's name is a secret.
Y   aks moo at you.
Z   ookeepers keep an eye on you.

Lucy Denton (8)
Horbury Bridge CE JI Primary School

THE CHRISTMAS TREE

The
sparkling
star on top
of the tree.
The tinsel scattered
all over. Stockings
hung on the tree.
Fairy lights have been
put on, flashing bulbs
on the bottom of the tree. The
little angel singing to me.

Paige Mitchell (8)
Horbury Bridge CE JI Primary School

THE SEA AND THE STORM

The thunder is roaring.
The lightning is crashing.
The lightning is flashing,
Against the rocks beside the sea.

The sea is rough.
The sea is wild.
The sea is tough,
Like an angry bear.

Charlotte Rawden (9)
Horbury Bridge CE JI Primary School

The Football

The football all round
It is in the hands of you
You kick it
See if you score
As you dribble it along the floor
Somebody shoots
Is it in?
No, you saved it!
Good job.

Bradley Gearey (9)
Horbury Bridge CE JI Primary School

School

A pencil is like a murderer's knife,
The mobiles are bats flapping about,
The caretaker is a vampire peering shadow to shadow,
The teachers are mindless zombies looking for victims,
The TV is an evil eye staring at you,
School's a really scary place at night.

Damian Brayshaw (10)
Horbury Bridge CE JI Primary School

Mary Had A Little, Little Lamb

Mary had a little lamb,
Its fleece was ocean-blue
And everywhere the lamb went,
It left a trail of glue.

Thomas Leyshon (9)
Horbury Bridge CE JI Primary School

ANIMAL ALPHABET

A nts crawl around you.
B aboons glare and stare at you.
C aterpillars creep around you.
D ogs bark at you.
E lephants spray water at you.
F rogs jump up and scare you.
G rasshoppers hop for you.
H orses buck and it hurts you.
I nsects buzz and fly around you.
J aguars climb around you.
K angaroos jump for you.
L eopards stare at you.
M onkeys swing on branches for you.
N ewts splash you.
O ctopi catch you with long arms.
P arrots squawk at you.
Q uails flap at you.
R abbits jump and scratch you.
S nakes slither towards you.
T ortoise move slowly towards you.
U nicorns don't exist for you.
V enomous snakes hiss at you.
W hales splash and wet you.
X there isn't one, so next . . .
Y aks spit at you.
Z ookeepers watch you.

Kirsty Robinson (8)
Horbury Bridge CE JI Primary School

DINNER TIME

D elicious dinner waiting for me.
I can't wait for 12 o'clock.
N ine o'clock still waiting.
N ine dinners just for me.
E ating my scrumptious dinner.
R acing to the queue.

T ime for dinner.
I am having pizza.
M e hungry, me hungry,
E ating delicious dinner.

Ryan Verity (9)
Horbury Bridge CE JI Primary School

MONSTERS

M onsters are greedy.
O gres are ugly and fierce.
N ight-time screams.
S noring monsters in the night.
T rees rustling in the darkness.
E ating people.
R oaring in the trees.
S neaking up on you.

Laura Madden (9)
Horbury Bridge CE JI Primary School

PENALTY

The ball's on the spot,
Your heart is beating like a drum.
The goalie is looking like a fierce warrior,
You step back,
The referee blows his whistle,
You kick the ball powerfully,
The goalie dives the wrong way,
Goal! The crowd goes wild.

Jamie Lamont (10)
Horbury Bridge CE JI Primary School

DOWN BY THE SEA

Down by the sea,
Down by the sea,
Soggy seaweed slides,
Shimmering sand shifting,
Silly seagulls singing,
Wet cliffs crumble,
Down by the sea,
Down by the sea,
Darting dolphins singing like silly seagulls.

Eleanor Mitchell (9)
Horbury Bridge CE JI Primary School

ANGER

I've had a fight with my sister,
'Cause she made me feel red,
But I got told off,
'Cause I whacked her round the head.

I got sent to my room
And she laughed at me,
I felt angry inside
'Cause I wasn't allowed my tea.

When I got told off,
I felt really bad,
So I said sorry to my sister,
For acting really mad.

I had another fight with my sister,
But she got done instead,
Then she nicked my remote control
And she got sent to bed!

Emily Schofield (10)
Horbury Bridge CE JI Primary School

WAITING FOR LUNCH

My tummy rumbles as I wait for lunch,
Five minutes to go, Miss, please let us out for lunch.
We've been angels all morning!

Three minutes to go, please Miss, I'm starving to death.

Lunchtime at last! Thank goodness for that!

Aletia Harper (9)
Horbury Bridge CE JI Primary School

MY ROOM

My room is dark,
I hate it all,
Except for my bed,
Cos it's cosy and small.

My room is cold and spooky,
It's scary and gloomy,
But my bed is safe and secure
And that's for sure.

Hannah Denton (9)
Horbury Bridge CE JI Primary School

SNAILS

Snail munching,
Snail crunching at my plants,
Snail glittering in the sun,
Snail sliding slowly through the grass,
Snail leaving a shiny silver trail,
Snail slides slowly,
Snail looks at me in its whirlpool,
Snail does its own thing,
In its own world.

Rachel Walls (10)
Horbury Bridge CE JI Primary School

FRACTIONS

Fractions, fractions, boring old fractions,
There's no great attractions
In doing boring fractions.

Fractions, fractions, boring old fractions,
Give me some subtractions
Instead of doing fractions.

Fractions, fractions, boring old fractions,
Give me some distractions
From these horrible fractions.

Fractions, fractions, boring old fractions,
There's no great attractions
In doing boring fractions.

Amy Cudworth (10)
Horbury Bridge CE JI Primary School

WORLD WAR II

At the start of World War II
Hitler began to build up his crew
One by one he added them on
Some were weak and some were strong
England heard about all of this
Which only made them clench their fists
On and on went the war
Everything got worse including the gore
But in the end, you know the story
England won all the *glory!*

Herbie Naylor-Mayers (10)
Horbury Bridge CE JI Primary School

MY SISTER

My sister is only four years old,
She never does as she's told.
Her name is Georgia Ebony Grainger,
She's full of mischief, often in danger.

She is very, very annoying
And she's always destroying.
She trips up every minute
And she pushes my mum to the limit.

She can be fun when she's in a good mood
And she is very picky with her food.
She chatters all day,
In a funny kind of way
And I'm about to say,
She's the *best sister ever!*

Cheyenne Grainger (9)
Inglebrook School

FAVOURITE THINGS

My favourite colour is blue,
My favourite band is Blue.
I like the songs they do,
Especially when they sing boo.

Riding is my favourite hobby,
Galloping on Blaze or Filly
Is the best thing I can do.
But when it's time to stop,
I put on a different top,
Give them both some hay,
Then go out to play.

Laura Pindar (9)
Inglebrook School

I LOVE TO PRETEND

When I play at cafes, serving is the best
With my dolls for customers, they sit and have a rest
Cappuccino, shokolatte, hot fudge cake and cream
The menu is indulgent, the desserts are just a dream

Mum brought home some brochures, just to take a look
Suddenly my bedroom became a Thomas Cook!
'Yes Sir, can I help you? A free child place you need.'
With shoebox for computer, I'm sure I will succeed

For Christmas I was given a microphone with stand
Wearing my new jacket, shades and trilby in my hand
I became a real pop star singing to a tune
Stardom, limos, flashing lights, it couldn't come too soon

I get some inspiration from Children's BBC
'Hello and welcome to Smart with PVA Pete, Charcoal Cliff and me
To make a groovy handbag that sparkles in the street
Sew sequins onto stripy felt and now it is complete!'

Cafes, Thomas Cook, pop stars and PVA Pete
These are all people you couldn't wish to meet
It's only imagination that's stored in my head
Another day is over and now it's time for bed!

Jenny Barker (9)
Inglebrook School

MY SCHOOL

School's boring, it's like a jail
In my exams I always fail

In games I am a little bit naughty
And I always get told off by Miss Sporty

My friend's the teacher's pet
And she never gets upset

We charge about outside with a ball
Sometimes we have food fights in the hall

The food is scattered on the floor
Of course the Head walks through the door!

Detention!

Charlotte Bennett (9)
Inglebrook School

ME

My name is Alice,
I would like to live in a palace.
I like to play football,
I wish my dad owned a stall.

My worst fear is guns,
My favourite food is buns.
My favourite football team is Leeds,
I like making necklaces out of beads.

I'm quite clever at school,
But sometimes I can be a fool.
My worst subject is maths,
I like going to the swimming baths.

Alice Sandham (9)
Inglebrook School

MY PETS

First of all I had some fish
They lived in a little dish
We put them in my grandma's pond
Until they died in the freezing cold

Secondly I had a rabbit
And then I started my little habit
Of giving it jam and bread
He got too fat, next he was dead

Thirdly I have some dogs
They like chasing frogs
I take them for a walk each day
And then we go back to play.

Olivia Shelton (10)
Inglebrook School

HOBBIES

I love ice skating
It's my favourite hobby
My other favourite is art
Especially when it's splodgy
And other things too
I think football's dodgy
My worst thing is tennis
It's what I wouldn't like to do
Best of all is riding
Because it's very fast
Time just flashes past
As I go galloping by
And when I get off, I sigh.

Sophie Astle (10)
Inglebrook School

PETS

What beautiful pets
Cats, bats and even rats

What beautiful pets you are, you are
What beautiful pets you are

I love my pets
Cats rolling up in a ball
Fluffy and colourful, all
Even when I am sure
I love them even more
My cat kisses me goodnight
Curls up in a ball so tight
I love all pets but best of all
I love my hamster, grey and small
I called her Betty and fed her until
she was so full she became ill
I took her and hugged her goodbye
I put her back in her cage to die.

Ashley Elliott (9)
Inglebrook School

I HAVE A FRIEND

I have a friend who laughed when I fell
I have a friend who pushed me down a well
I have a friend who held me high
I have a friend who made me cry
I have a friend who sprayed me with a hose
I have a friend with a freckled nose
Despite all this, I have to say
She'll be my friend till my dying day.

Naomi Knaggs (10)
Inglebrook School

BANG!

I was on Earth
And a lady gave birth
She gave birth to a boy
He killed joy
He was called Dennis
He was a menace
He killed joy with a *bang*
Every day he talked slang
He talked slang to everyone

He tricked with a whoopee cushion
And he pulled off people's buttons
He kept on hitting
He was always spitting
Spitting at everyone
Then he said, 'Done!'
He pulled out his tongue
Everyone cried for their mum
All the mums told him off

Then he went home
Brushed his hair with a comb
And then he went to bed
He said in his head
I'm getting up
And then he tripped up
And his mum threw him out of the door.

Rachel Cook (9)
Inglebrook School

PETS

Pets are fun,
Best of all is a dog,
It barks all night long.
When I get up,
He jumps up at me
And pushes me over.
But sometimes I wish
Someone would come
And take him away,
For a week or a day.

A gerbil is not much fun,
All it does is eat
And sleep and sleep,
With its fluffy fur,
Soft, like a teddy bear.

A kitten has fun
With a piece of wool,
It will play all day
With a bundle of hay,
Pets are the best.

Hadley Stringer (10)
Inglebrook School

TIME IS JUST TIME

Tick-tock, that's time,
Some are in mines,
Some are at home,
Some people have clocks when they're alone,
But time is just time.

Some people have clocks,
Some people have locks,
Most people have doors,
Some people live in the moors,
But time is just time.

Some people have watches,
Some people have matches,
Some people like opening latches,
But time is just time.

Andrew Earnshaw (9)
Inglebrook School

THE FUNFAIR

Once I went to the fair,
I had a very big scare.
In the Big Top I sat
On a very small cat
And the clown had very big hair.

I went in the House of Fun,
I sunbathed in the sun.
I bumped into a pillar
And broke a big mirror
And now I'm feeling all numb.

Christopher Speight (10)
Inglebrook School

THE NEVER-ENDING ROLLER COASTER

Once I went on a roller coaster
It was the biggest in the world
It had loops, twists and turns
And other things out of this world

First it went up really high
I thought I was going to die
It made me feel really ill
And my dad made me take a pill.

Thomas Hicks (9)
Inglebrook School

MY SHELL

I found a shell upon a beach,
It was big and twisted.
I put it to my ear,
This is what I heard . . .
My shell took me to a sandy shore,
Calm, turquoise waters,
A bright golden sun like a rosette.

Wavy grass on the cliff,
A tiny craggy island,
A crowded bay with lots of swimming people,
A swaying tide.

I felt the gentle breeze on my face,
The soft sand on my feet,
My shell is cool!

Edward Grayson (8)
Larks Hill JI School

THE SPIRAL SHELL

My teacher gave some shells out; I put one to my ear,
There is the sea and there is the pier,
The wind is sleeping,
I feel calm at this place and I like it,
Kids are listening to the shells, which are spiral,
Like some stairs,
The sea is swaying gently,
To and fro,
Some shells are big
And some are really small!
Bang went the thunder,
Clash went the rain,
I don't like it here now,
All the ships are shipwrecking,
But then . . .
I took the shell away,
Now I'm back at *school!*

Emily Carr (8)
Larks Hill JI School

SHELL

Starfish feel like sand
Takes me to a hotel at the seaside in France
I dig sand
Cold sand in the rain
Warm sand in the sun
The shells fill the holes
The waves of the sea
Suddenly I'm back at school.

Matthew Holmes (9)
Larks Hill JI School

SHELLS

I went to the beach for the first time this year
Walked on the sand to the sea
Found a tiny spiral shell
Put it to my ear
It took me to a tranquil, sunny place
Nobody knows about it
It's got white beaches
Huge cliffs
The tide is in
Fish swim around your legs
Palm trees swaying to and fro
To and fro
Dolphins leap in the tropical waters
I smell fruit germinating on high trees
I feel shells under my feet
I feel like a special person
I smell salty sea water
I took the shell away from my ear
I was bored again.

Hannah Young (9)
Larks Hill JI School

THE SHELL

I found a golden shell and placed it to my ear
I could hear the wind whistling
Lightning strikes across the seas
Sharks surround the creepy island
Fish swim briskly in the stormy seas
Rising, rolling tidal waves rush with the crisp wind.

Bradley Wilson (9)
Larks Hill JI School

THE SHELL

I have a shell
Just like a spiral
I'll put it to my ear and tell you my place
My place is stormy
Where the pebbles go to sea
A gale blows
Thunderclouds gather
I want to go back, I have to go on
Ships are rocking side to side
As the beam of the lighthouse scans the waves
The picture is blurring
I'll take the shell away
And listen no more.

Max Pepper (9)
Larks Hill JI School

THE SHELL

I look at my vivid shell and remember a beach
A sandy beach with children laughing
The smell of salt on the breeze

It reminds me of my other shells
It makes me think of home
It looks like it's got a nose
I listen to my shell, it sounds like sea

My shell is a pleasant shell
It is striped with outrageous orange lines
I hear the sea whispering to me.

Helena Wood (9)
Larks Hill JI School

THE PLACE IN MY SHELL

When I look at my shell
I am taken to a brilliantly sunny beach
On an uninhabited desert island
With a turquoise tropical ocean
Where I run
Underneath the palm trees
On golden sand
While the scorching sun blazes down
Onto the sea
Making it glisten like glitter
I can imagine my shell
Lying in the sand.

Matthew Riley (9)
Larks Hill JI School

TORNADO SHELL

My shell is like a tornado,
It takes me to a country that is in danger,
My shell can cause devastation,
I'm taken to a blazing desert in Egypt with golden sand
And silver reflections shining,
My shell is like a drill,
It takes me to a floor with mosaics all over it,
My shell is very scaly, a wood-brown,
My shell can exterminate buildings.

Liam Threlfall (9)
Larks Hill JI School

MY SHELL

As I harken to my shell,
It makes me feel that I'm in a nightmare,
It carries me to a place that's unloved
That's unsafe and uncared for
Crashing seas smash on rocks
Black pebbles invade the creamy sand
A wind whips across the harbour
Sharks hunt the bottom of the sea
Shells are chipped and broken
Splintered wood drifts from shipwrecked boats
The moon hides behind dark clouds
The tide sleeps coldly
Eagles are shrieking in the air
Rocks are carved with weird signs
Waves make pictures, they splash
As I look back my footprints are gone
I return the shell to its resting place
And I'm taken back to the 21st century.

Andrew Parry (8)
Larks Hill JI School

SPECIAL

My shell is special,
It takes me away
To a sandy island on a
Summer's day.
I listen to the sea crashing
Against the harbour wall
And think of the waves tickling my toes.

Sophie Lambert (8)
Larks Hill JI School

THE SHELL

I found a shell, I put it to my ear
I heard the sea splashing
Upon the rock
There were lots of patterns on the shell
Shining gold and silver
It takes me to a sunny shore
With seaweed on the soggy sand
I see crabs on the pebbles
Fish swimming beside them
Out in the distance there are boats
Sailing on the sparkling sea
Then I take the shell from my ear
And I am back at school.

Joshua Atkinson (9)
Larks Hill JI School

THE SHELL

This shell is freezing inside,
It looks like a drill,
My shell makes me think of
The hermit crab that
Wore it on its back.
I put it to my ear,
I hear sea crashing on the rocks,
Quickly I take it away,
I am pleased to be home.

Joshua Metcalfe (9)
Larks Hill JI School

MY SPECIAL SHELL

This special shell is like a sunset
Pearly white inside
Takes me to a tropical desert island
With whispering tides
Waves glisten
Like the stars in the midnight sky

The scorching sun blazes down
Multicoloured birds fly
High up in the canopy

I feel relaxed and safe
All my friends around me
Fruit dangling for us all to eat
I put my shell down
I was home watching boring TV again.

Madeleine Prew (8)
Larks Hill JI School

THE SEASIDE SHELL

My shell takes me to a beach
The tide is in
I start to paddle in the sea
I bend down and pick a shell up
And all day long I have good luck
I carry the shell everywhere I go
I see palm trees
Swaying to and fro, to and fro
Multicoloured parrots flying from the treetops
But unfortunately it is all a dream.

Elizabeth Haddington (8)
Larks Hill JI School

MY SHELL

When I walk across a beach
And when I find a good-looking, gleaming shell
I place it to my ear
This is where I'm taken
I'm taken to a tropical island
With the sea lapping on the beach
Where oranges, mangos and pears grow
I watch the turquoise ocean
Splashing all around me
I smell the scent of the salty sea
The juicy fruit and the dry sand
And when I put it down, I'm back at home
Being shouted by my mum.

Christopher Harris (9)
Larks Hill JI School

SHELL

I trip over something at the beach
I see a shell, I listen to it
This shell whisks me to a place
Where the sea is thundery-blue
The wind breezy, swaying, swishing, raw, shivery and perishing
The waves are invincible, impregnable
Unconquerable and unbreakable
The sun is invisible and unnoticeable
My shell looks like a castle on a cliff
I put it on the ground and there wasn't a sound.

Kalon Everitt (9)
Larks Hill JI School

My Adventure

I am walking on a beach
I'm on my holidays
I find a shell
It looks like an ice cream
I like the look of it
I pick it up and hold it to my ear
Shut my eyes and imagine the place my shell takes me to
It is a dim, shadowy, gloomy place
I can hear a thunderstorm coming
I feel cheerless, disappointed, joyless
Because nobody will know this place
Now I put my shell down
And I am back on a happy, cheerful beach.

Rosanna Loftus (8)
Larks Hill JI School

Shell

On a beach I found a shell
I placed it to my ear
Immediately transported
To a frosty, lonely place
Winds whistle while
Thunder claps
Waves crash
Slimy seaweed creeps onto the shore
Boats pitch side to side
To and fro
I took the shell away from my ear
I was happy
To go home.

Chloe Mylonas (8)
Larks Hill JI School

MY BEACH

My shell takes me to a beach with wind gusting
Rock pools, dull shells, jagged edges
The wind blows sand across me
The sea is cold around my ankles
My beach is no place to play

Shells hide behind rocks
Rough on top
Smooth inside
Bronze, tiny and jagged
A swirl of wind
Whips the sand into spirals
My beach is no place to play

Short shells
Long shells
Fat and thin shells
Lay alone
Homes of creatures
My beach is no place to play

Storms swathe
Sun is screened by clouds
Lightning strikes
Thunder crashes
My beach is no place to play.

Heather Lindsay (8)
Larks Hill JI School

SCARY SHELL

This shell takes me to a lonely place
It is cold
I can hear the waves pouncing
Rough, dark
I can see the sand blowing in a spiral
It is scary, creepy
I feel frightened.

Ben Chappell (8)
Larks Hill JI School

THE SHELL

My shell is shaped like an ice cream cone
Takes me to a happy beach
The sun is beaming down
The sea shimmers
I go closer to the shimmering water.

Alicia Lemm
Larks Hill JI School

MY SHELL

This shell takes me to a sunny sandy beach
With a turquoise glistening sea
Stretching far out into the immense world
Hermit crabs scuttling across the shore
Children licking cold ice cream, melting in the sun
Waves come rushing up and down the shore
Mums and dads are sunbathing on the glittery sand
This is where the shell takes me.

Jessica Adlington (9)
Larks Hill JI School

MY SHELL

I see a shell with something inside
I think it's a hermit crab that is moving out
I quickly pick up the shell
I put it by my ear
The noise takes me to a swishy sea
Sharp rocks fall off the cliff
The tide comes in
I am getting wet
I take the shell away from my ear
The sun is shining after all.

Matthew Lindsay (8)
Larks Hill JI School

SHELLS

Those shells take me to a beach with happy people
Watching shells and all the little sea creatures
All the lovely fish in the sea
All the interesting fish down in the depths of the ocean
My shell is sharp at the end like a unicorn
Pale like ivory
It takes me to Mother Nature
Like the hawk diving down to capture its prey
A shell that is like a teacup
Those shells make me feel joyful and happy.

Christopher Walker (9)
Larks Hill JI School

MY SHELL

This place my shell takes me
Has twisted jagged rocks
A sea bursting with colourful creatures
Spiral sandcastles
And lots of shipwrecks
Bumpy crabs running
Side to side
White clouds soft and fluffy
Tiny clams scared stiff
Skies turquoise
Golden orange sun
The slow whisper of the sea.

Ryan James Langley (8)
Larks Hill JI School

SHELL

It reminds me of a sandy beach
I can feel smoothness
I can feel bumps
I can feel spiky sharp points
Its colour is orangey-yellow
It is stripy
And holey
My shell makes me free
I can hear the sea.

Sarah Vause (9)
Larks Hill JI School

MY SHELL

Walking along a beach
Gazing at waves lapping my toes
Something catches my eye
A beautiful spiral shell
It took me to a frosty, freezing, shivering place
My shell is like a kite
Flying in the breezy air
It takes me to the seaside
People's hair blows to and fro, to and fro
Children build sandcastles
I smell the salty sea water
I hear the sea swaying back and forth
The whispering tide comes to me
I feel lonely, I feel cold and want to go home to the warmth
I hope I never go back!

Lana Hopkins (9)
Larks Hill JI School

THE SHELL

My shell is bumpy,
Reminds me of a stormy deserted beach,
It looks like a spiral,
Spinning around,
Then I think about the creature
That lived in it before,
Could it be a crab
Or a cockle?

Georgina Myers (8)
Larks Hill JI School

MY SHELL

My shell takes me to a place
Where you can hear the tide coming up
I can see a crab snapping its claws
A fish swimming in a rock pool
A palm tree swaying to and fro.

Christopher Gill (8)
Larks Hill JI School

AUTUMN'S ARRIVAL

When autumn arrives,
Trees stand bare,
Branches wither
And insects march to their homes.
The wind comes,
Annihilating the leaves,
Destroying everything in its way.
With its mean claws
And its venomous teeth, it
Bites the leaves,
Bites the bark,
Slices the leaves,
Which tumble
From the trees;
And golden tears
Plummet from the sky.

Peter Green (10)
Malsis School

SNOW

Crisp snow lies all around;
Dagger-like icicles hang dangerously from branches.
Grinning faces all around;
Crystal cold snowmen
Smile then cry. The
Glinting hair on bushes
Gleams brightly as a deadly white blanket
Kills every plant in its path, and
Icy claws grip little children's hands.

William Leigh-Bramwell (9)
Malsis School

THE SEA

The sea is
A serpent slithering up
The beach,
Hissing as the
Waves thump
The defenceless
Cliffs.
It is
A python secretly snatching shells,
Hoarding and hiding them,
Hungry no more.
He lies motionless,
Deep down in the depths;
Watching and waiting.

Antonia Benson (11)
Malsis School

THE FUNERAL

Flowers hang miserably on railings,
Rays of sun glow
Through stained glass windows.
Dark clouds cry
Sad tears and
Trees weep with grief.
People step slowly down
The aisle;
Coins clang in the shiny
Gold pot; the coffin
Gleams in the beaming
Candlelight; while
People sway
Sadly, as they pray.

Charlotte Warburton (11)
Malsis School

SNOW

Behind the curtains
The trees ache with frostbite,
Unable to stop its pain.
It is white everywhere:
The grass covered with a white blanket,
Keeping it cold,
While the wind whispers,
Blowing bushes with white hair.

Jonathan Hutchinson (10)
Malsis School

SNOW

The glittering glow
Of the glaring sun
Kills the white people,
While cold clouds wail.
White, snowy tears mournfully, and
The white shadow suffocates
The peaceful animals.
Mountains stand still
Like skeletons, until
The deadly sun strikes again.

Xavier Greenwood (8)
Malsis School

A MERMAID'S KINGDOM

It roars with anger
And never says goodbye
It spits rudely
And mutters to itself
It throws surfers off;
It growls
Opening its mouth
And tries to bite
Its white hair is uncombed
And falls out in the sun.

Sophie McMullan (9)
Malsis School

WIND

Trees sway sadly
Like old men;
Clouds chase the sun,
Like obedient servants
To the wind king.
He bites angrily
And children run quickly,
Screaming for shelter.
Flowers dance
Crazily to and fro;
While clouds turn dark,
Animals go home
And the wind
Noisily runs away.

Jessica Bailey (11)
Malsis School

WINTER'S WORLD

Frost freezes frightened grass,
Leaves die,
Suffocated from the smothering snow.
Fog engulfs the sky
Like a blanket of wonderful white;
Slithers of sunshine beam down, and
The ground twinkles like diamonds on fingers.
Frozen lakes crack;
As the world wakes,
Ears turn ravenous red and
Winter wanders through the world.

Todd Robinson (10)
Malsis School

CHRISTMAS

Christmas is cracking fun,
Opening presents from everyone,
Decorating the Christmas tree,
Everybody's waiting, like me!

Lights flashing all around,
Carols making a merry sound,
Turkey, sprouts and Christmas pud,
I would eat it all, if I could!

Seeing my aunty and her great big tree,
Lots of chatting between her and me,
Nanny always joins us too,
With her knitted jumpers, red, green and blue!

Everyone full of Christmas cheer,
Now it's all over, can't wait for next year!

Harry Warburton (9)
Malsis School

SNOW

It is like a freezing blanket
Trying to suffocate the Earth.
Old, tall trees shiver silently
In the crystal covered snow, and
Houses smoke their cigarettes.
Cold water still, as hard stone,
And trees look like mountains
With cold, snowy tops.

Charles Farnes (9)
Malsis School

A SHARK'S RESTAURANT

Huge white waves surround the beach,
Surfers thrown off surfboards
Into the hungry wild water.
The tide destroys deckchairs
As if they were just pieces of paper.
Waves slap solid rocks
On the edge of the beach,
While ships drown helplessly
And sink into the depths
Where some monstrous jaws
Swallow everything -
Its hunger satisfied.

Jonathan Wells (9)
Malsis School

THE SEA

The sea, smooth, shiny
Like a cat sleeping
On the golden
Carpet of sand.
But when
Disturbed
It becomes a tiger,
Roaring at the rocks;
Its white paws
Clawing at the sand,
Tossing its head in anger
But soon it is
Tired and breathless
And sleeps.

Nicole Dadhley (9)
Malsis School

A SURFER'S PARADISE

The sea roars loudly,
It crashes at rocks rudely;
The rocks spit back.
A shipwreck washes into the harbour,
The boat arrives
And wives cry with joy -
Fish is piled up high;
A feast tonight.
The sea smiles gently;
A friend today, but tomorrow . . .
It roars loudly
At the white horses.

Edward Smith (9)
Malsis School

AUTUMN

Wind whirls round,
Trees wave and dance in time
With the green grass;
Rain tumbles and thumps
On the quilted ground, and
The sun waits like a dog
Waiting for his dinner.
Rain gallops down
On the battered bark of the tree
While winds whirl dangerously
Round the naked trees.

Henry Brook (11)
Malsis School

THE BONFIRE

There's a huge wild beast in my field,
Flailing its flaming arms;
Pushing and crunching
Its jaws together;
Snapping its excited legs;
Kicking angrily at the armour of a tree.
It whips its tongue cumbersomely
In the cool air,
Cackling at every passer-by.
Its breath crawls up an old oak tree,
Its tongue following after.
It climbs the tree,
Not feeling the branches
On its shimmering shoulders,
Its nimble feet running through the rough leaves,
Only needing to glare at them to scare them away.
It eats too much, it begins to grow,
It gets so angry, its hair sticks up.
Its face goes red;
It scorches the grass,
Turning boxes and wardrobes into dust.
It burns and it burns
And it burns all night, until morning,
When it sleeps in a flutter of ashes.

Nicholas Thompson (9)
Malsis School

THE FUNERAL

The sombre soldier stands
Like a statue -
His burnished
Buttons glisten in the
Dwindling light; silent
Mourners shuffle
Slowly past the
Altar -
Bow their heads. Silence
Embraces the room -
A veil
Smothering all noise;
As mourners pay
Their last respects to
Our nation's
Grandmother.

Joshua Greenwood (11)
Malsis School

SNOW

The snow clings onto the grass;
Houses cover themselves with white blankets,
Snowmen cry as the beaming sun shines
At their round faces.
Shouting children chuck
Freezing cold snowballs,
Wearing woolly jumpers.
Jack Frost strangles
Shivering grass,
Suffocating in the brightness.

James Healey (9)
Malsis School

Rain

Sitting, I gaze through the window,
Hypnotised by falling raindrops;
Just rain not even snow,
Lazily dancing in the air,
Not fussed where they land,
Splashing into puddles,
When they do, watching silently,
I was buried in dismay -
Continuously, water poured down
From the sky,
Trapping me,
Surrounding me by frowns of glass:
My happiness is drowned away.

Bryony Harrap (11)
Malsis School

Snow

The white, wispy snow tumbles excitedly
To the powdery ground,
Grasping white-haired bushes.
Gripping tightly,
The wind whispers
And trees shake their heads;
The white blanket crunches underfoot,
The cold gnawing at swollen red fingers, as
The white snow disappears
And green grass slowly glows through.

Jennifer Slack (9)
Malsis School

THE BONFIRE

There's a colossal brute
In the field,
Ablaze and distressed,
Fighting at the nagging army
Of sizzled leaves.
His black breath climbs heavily
Into the red sky,
His arms frantically tossing about
Like a bird.
In the sky, he bellows out,
Destroying the wood with a crack!
His fury and excitement rise -
He is fed more
And more,
Until hungry no longer -
Soon he sleeps in ashes;
His long arms still at last.

Freddy Hammond (11)
Malsis School

SNOW

The soft powdery snow
Freezes the world
With its frighteningly cold blood;
The children come excitedly out,
Build snowmen -
But before long
Laughter turns to tears,
And they melt away
Under the great glittering sun.
The Earth cries as the sun smiles.

Elliott Bell (9)
Malsis School

FOOT AND MOUTH

The invisible killers -
They target the innocent - elect their victims.
Anxious farmers prepare their undesirable future.
Unpleasant odours from burning carcasses pollute the air.
Motionless figures lie rigid, upturned:
Ready to burn.
Waiting, the time will arrive -
They leave none alive.
Ghosts of the dead appear through burning smoke:
Come to haunt the lives of the fortunate.
Soon, few will remain;
All will be gone.
Their main intention has been said:
To leave them dead.

Sarah Naylor (11)
Malsis School

THE HORSES

Far away, howling wind bites their feeble fur:
The echoing crunch of iron-shod hooves,
Billowing clouds of breath,
Cocked left hind shoes.
Short grasses of the cold valley
Which dance with wind, they chew.
Restless snow swirls on the hilltop
Touching, chilling, freezing all,
Even the shaggy mane atop
Their long sleek necks;
Tongues drink the dewdrops,
As the horses stand the winter.

Andrew Denman (11)
Malsis School

SNOW

The snow strangles the lovely trees
As well as cutting throats.
You see its shadow creeping behind
On the silver, slippy, skaty ice.
It hides our beautiful wonders
Under its woolly white blanket.

Vanessa Bailey (9)
Malsis School

SNOW

The white snow grips angrily to the bushes;
The excited frost nibbles your hand
Like a hamster gnaws its food.
The tearful snowman cries
As the smiling sun melts him,
And he slowly shrinks -
A baby again.

Jacey Rawsthorne (9)
Malsis School

THE SEASIDE

The sun beams down at the soft cool sand;
Water horses charge angrily
Through blue fields.
The evil wind stretches his arms
And sucks the water from the horses;
They plummet to the sea below them,
Then wait till next summer's first day.

Jack Starr (11)
Malsis School

A Trip In The Dark

A rattle; a bang!
My feet froze.
I tried to become free, but
The gate outside clashed closed;
I jumped,
Then listened.
Smash!
I edged out nervously;
Darkness clung to me,
Suffocating me,
Not letting me go.
The walls gave out a scream of laughter.
The coldness
Anchored my feet to the ground.
Who would save me now?

Rabia Qureshi (10)
Malsis School

Autumn Wind

The starving tall tree
Shivers and cries golden tears,
Bowing to the mighty wind.
The leaves dance with joy -
They are free!
The whistling wind
Whispers to the green leaves
'Die, die, die!'

Christopher Gliniecki (10)
Malsis School

WINTER'S MORNING

On a cold
Christmas morning
Grey smoke was scrambling
From the old mansion's chimney
Which was breathing for life.
The ice-rink glitters like pearls;
Aged bushes wear a wig of white hair,
While branches grasp like hands,
Their cruel fingers clutch snowballs
And then throw them like rubbish.
Red fingers freeze,
And the world turns to white.

Charlie Pilkington (9)
Malsis School

THE SEASIDE

Waves hammer at the shore,
The stuttering wind
Bites the ocean,
Roaring, surging like
A lion against its prey.
Greedy goblins
Look for ice cream,
The sun ravenously licks
People's skin,
Children laugh and cry
Like clashing waves;
Deckchairs creak and chink
And sandcastles melt
As the sun devours its prey.

Ramit Abrol (11)
Malsis School

THE SEASIDE

Waves attack the shore barbarically
While the wind roars at the harmless crooked rocks;
Children run rapidly
Howling for ice cream, while
Mums play dead
As the sun smiles evilly
Planning a slow, red torture.
Ice cream queues
Slither round corners
Like a snake, as the sea roars.

Charles Naylor (10)
Malsis School

THE SEASIDE

The sun shines silently
On the defenceless sand,
The wind wails and
The hungry sea gobbles up
Anyone in its path.
To the edge of the calm cool beach,
Mums play dead
While children moan and groan;
And cafes welcome
Hungry, ravenous people
Into its den.

Anthony Ingham (10)
Malsis School

WINTER'S MORNING

Teeth chatter;
Frost tears at my body
Like an angry lion,
Ice smothering lakes,
The cold rips through coats,
My breath rises in a mist before me;
Bushes have white layers draped over them,
While early morning birds sing like a choir,
Children lick icicles like lollipops,
As the world disappears.

Alex Ickringill (10)
Malsis School

THE SEASIDE

Wind sweeps empty beaches,
Gradually gobbling people's picnics.
The starving sea sprints furiously
At defenceless children, and
Rocks drown;
Babies scream while mums act dead
Under the fierce sun;
Scavenging seagulls eat
Until they are full,
While boys slide on sand hills
And destroy sandcastles.

Joseph Webster (11)
Malsis School

SEASIDE

Waves slash against the lazy soft sand,
Like a lion catching its prey.
The bright greedy sun
Gobbles away at the seaweed;
Breezes starve,
Waiting for their next victim to appear.
Seagulls hover overhead like robbers
Waiting to steal;
And fish swim lazily in the sea.

Ollie Greenwood (10)
Malsis School

FROST

Frost dashes through the
Winter wonderland
Like an Olympic sprinter.
Icicles dangle, deadly
From the tree's tentacles,
Hanging on for their lives.
The wind howls
As Jack Frost
Suffocates everything,
Engulfing the ground
In a soft blanket of white;
Freezing frightened life.

Todd Robinson (10)
Malsis School

HARRY POTTER

It was Harry's first year at Hogwarts,
His head was buzzing with thoughts,
He sat on the stool and after that,
They put on his head an old, tatty hat.

He wondered 'witch' team he was in,
Gryffindor, Hufflepuff, Ravenclaw, Slytherin,
The hat shouted out, 'Gryffindor',
He jumped with delight and ran to the door.

Mrs McGonagall came outside,
Grabbed his wrist and took him inside,
She told Wood, 'You've got a new seeker,'
When Harry told Ron, he looked a bit weaker.

Harry went to his first Quidditch match,
Wood told Harry that he must catch
The golden ball, called the snitch,
He warned him not to fall in a ditch.

He got on his broomstick and flew around a bit more,
It was Gryffindor Vs Ravenclaw,
They had won the game within ten minutes time,
The total score was 150 to 9.

They found a door to a three-headed dog,
Jumped into the trapdoor and got stuck in a bog,
They went through 5 chambers or so,
But at the end, Harry defeated his foe.

They all hopped onto the train,
As it was starting to rain,
The train set off and went round the bend
And that was the very end.

Alexandra Bacon (10)
Mill Dam JI School

MAN UNITED

M an United are great
A ll the players are mates
N ever let Alex Ferguson down
C hase the ball all the time
H ave always tried their best
E very match they play home or away
S o great, I like them so much
T ry all the time
E ach game they try to win
R ev up all the time to win

U nbeaten for eight runs
N ever give up hope
I nternational football they play
T wo days they face Arsenal
E ach game they play, they play their best
D oing their best all the time.

Nathan Morgan (9)
Mill Dam JI School

ANIMALS

A horse is soft and tame
A donkey is great to ride on
A dog is fun to play with
A puppy is cute and fluffy
A cat is warm to cuddle with
And a kitten is lovely to sleep with.

Alaina Everson (8)
Mill Dam JI School

POPEYE

He's Popeye the sailor man,
He lives in a caravan,
He went to the pictures
And pulled down his breeches,
He's Popeye the sailor man.
He's Popeye the sailor man,
He lives in a caravan,
He went to the fair
And lost all of his hair,
He's Popeye the sailor man.
He's Popeye the sailor man,
He lives in a caravan,
He went to the beach
And got sucked by a leech,
He's Popeye the sailor man.

Oliver Hemingway Brooke (8)
Mill Dam JI School

BRAZIL

Brazil, Brazil gives the other team a sleeping pill,
Ronaldo scores a goal,
Hits the ball past Cole
And Rivaldo hits the post,
Goes on holiday to the coast,
Roberto Carlos takes a free kick
Hits Seaman like a brick.

Chris Paterson (8)
Mill Dam JI School

MY CLASS

I love the way Jack moves his eyes.
I love the way Chris spikes his hair.
I love Alaina's American accent.
I love the way Charlotte writes.
I love the way Oliver takes me seriously.
I love the way Jordan makes me laugh.
I love the way Thomas runs around like a total idiot.
I love Katherine's hairdo.
I love the way Mr Hodgekiss plays his guitar.
I love the way Rebecca plays her violin.
I love the way Nathan draws
And I love the way everybody is themselves.

Samantha Taylor (9)
Mill Dam JI School

HARRY POTTER

Harry Potter the famous wizard,
Stirs up magic with a whiz and a blizzard.
Ron, Hermione of course not alone,
Out on a search for the Philosopher's Stone.
On the way, a game of giant wizard's chess
A dangerous game more or less.
After hours of searching, the stone is found
And safely returned to Hogwarts' ground.
A huge celebration, a giant feast,
The Philosopher's Stone has been released!

Francesca Ellis (11)
Mill Dam JI School

HULLABALOO AT HOME

Saturday morning
7am
What a hullabaloo!
Rush hour's here!
We dash down the stairs
And get dressed in our compartments
Rush to the town
Jae needs the toilet
Back again to our flat
Now we're flying again
To the town
Get shopping
Hurry, quick
We've finished, phew!
We walk back to the flat
Puffy-eyed and weak
Time for bed
What a hullabaloo!

Summer Lea Bedford (8)
North Featherstone JI School

HECTIC MORNINGS

Hectic mornings every rainy day,
Umbrellas up and out the door I go,
These days I hate in every way,
I go to school even if I feel low.
My hair is soaking when I arrive,
I sit with my clothes dripping.
I wish my mum could drive,
Then I would stop slipping.

Chantel Adamson (10)
North Featherstone JI School

HULLABALOO AT THE FOOTBALL PITCH

Saturday afternoon
What a hullabaloo
Players sprinting
Keeper diving
Crowd cheering
What a hullabaloo!

Defending, tackling
Fouls are coming in
Ref shouting
What a goal
Whistle blowing
Full time showing
What a hullabaloo!

Bradley Wood (9)
North Featherstone JI School

HULLABALOO

Saturday afternoon
At the fairground
What a hullabaloo!
Ferris wheel spinning
Children winning
Fathers grinning
Mum pinning her hopes on
Hook a duck

Roller coaster turning
Sun burning
Brother earning
What a hullabaloo . . . at the fair.

Daniel Parker (8)
North Featherstone JI School

HULLABALOO!

At the cinema
On cheap night
What a hullabaloo!
People queuing
Children moaning
'I'm bored'
One man working on his own
What a hullabaloo!

At the cinema
Getting sorted
What a hullabaloo
Popcorn flying
Mum's sighing
'Hurry up'
Finding seats
Getting drinks
Finally we're sorted
What a hullabaloo!

Ashleigh Olivia Davies (9)
North Featherstone JI School

HULLABALOO IN THE PLAYGROUND

In the playground,
Monday morning,
What a *hullabaloo!*
People crying,
Balls flying,
Girls lying,
All the teachers sighing,
People dashing, bashing and crashing,
What a hullabaloo!

Lunchtime break,
What a hullabaloo!
In the hall lots of people call,
After lunch . . .
Bullies punch.
Whistle goes,
Everything stops,
It blows again,
The rumble starts,
Children rushing,
Year 5s pushing,
The noisy lines fade away.

Thomas Garland-Jones (9)
North Featherstone JI School

WHAT A HULLABALOO!

In the playground
Morning break . . . what a hullabaloo!
Children running round and round
Chalking patterns on the ground
Dodging balls
Skipping ropes
Sad, happy
Who knows?

After lunch . . . playground rush hour
What a hullabaloo!
Mouths munching
Leaves crunching
Sweeping birds off their feet
Like a roller coaster dashing through the street
Moments later . . . the whistle blows
Silence!

Ellie Nicholson (8)
North Featherstone JI School

HULLABALOO!

The heart of *London*
It's rush hour
Cars rushing
People crashing
Children screaming
Shops crowding . . .
Tills ringing
Buildings filling
Boss shouting
What a hullabaloo!

James Browne (9)
North Featherstone JI School

HULLABALOO!

In the playground after lunch,
What a hullabaloo.
People running round and round,
Making noises on the ground,
Teachers standing and staring,
Making sure children are caring,
More teachers come striding out,
Find the children . . . then shout,
Boys lying, girls crying,
Year 6 girls screaming, boys beaming.
What a *hullabaloo!*

Paige Leach (9)
North Featherstone JI School

HULLABALOO!

In a football crowd
On a Saturday morning,
What a hullabaloo!
People flying,
Players lying
Beckham crying . . .
Football madness.

At full time,
No shirts shining,
Man U whining . . .
They refuse to lose.
What a hullabaloo!

David Blackburn (8)
North Featherstone JI School

HULLABALOO!

Driving through the London town,
It is a *hullabaloo* I have found.
When we get to the museum,
We dip and duck to get near,
When we get in, it's clear,
When we get through the door,
There is such a busy floor,
Mammals, dinosaurs and so much more,
We went on a tour,
It was a bit of a bore,
I saw a giant globe
And the law of gravity,
I peep and seek,
At the gift shop I earned my keep.

Alex Guy (8)
North Featherstone JI School

HULLABALOO!

In the computer room,
The computers have crashed,
What a hullabaloo!
Children moaning,
Teachers groaning,
Heat rising,
Tempers flying,
Machines humming,
Children waiting,
People praying . . .
The light clicks on,
They have woken up,
Computer heaven!

Laura Hunter (9)
North Featherstone JI School

HULLABALOO

At the end of school
It's a *hullabaloo!*
Pushing, shoving
Screaming, yelling
Coming, going
It's a *hullabaloo!*

On the corridor
Standing, chatting
Pushing to get through
Rushing to your packed lunch
In the cloakroom
Barging to your coat
Things falling from the hooks
It's crazy, it's terrible
Homework getting
Scrunched and muddy
Lost and all over the place
What a *hullabaloo!*

Coral Midgley (8)
North Featherstone JI School

HULLABALOO

There once was a boy with pace
Who entered in a school race
In a trice
He slipped on some ice
And landed smack bang on his face.

Adam Short (11)
North Featherstone JI School

HULLABALOO!

On holiday around the pool,
Splashing, dashing and crashing,
Screaming on the waterslide,
Suncream squirting all over the floor.
I can tell what this is . . .
A hullabaloo!
Ducking underwater,
Slippy paths too.
Wet footprints slapping the tiles too,
Wooden hotel doors slamming.
Fighting over sunbeds,
All this mayhem till noon.
When you're on holiday,
Go early so it won't be a case of
Hullabaloo!

Jessica Seaman (7)
North Featherstone JI School

ICY PLAYGROUND!

Slipping, sliding, skidding along
The playground's icy
'Come on! Come on!'
Children chanting
Snowball fights!
Yippee, yahoo
Let's skid in the lights –
It's getting cold
Now let's go home
Or else you'll end up
All alone.

Tiffany Bland (11)
North Featherstone JI School

HULLABALOO

In the playground
Where everybody is racing
And people are chasing
What a hullabaloo!

Footballs high
Footballs low
Where did that silly football go?

When children rush out for play
In that season it was May
They rush up out on the grass
What happens is . . .
They crash!

What a hullabaloo!
People playing skipping games
Or people playing *choo-choo* trains
When someone gets hurt
It is not a laugh

But when children fight
They might
Get sent to the Head
What a hullabaloo!

They argue
They fight
They give us a fright
What a hullabaloo!
They push
They shove
They wear one glove
Well most of the time . . .
What a hullabaloo!

Donna Marie Connelly (8)
North Featherstone JI School

98

HULLABALOO

Crystal ice,
Covers the ground,
Cold and icy,
On the playground.

Children slipping,
Skating, skipping,
Sliding, gliding,
On the playground.

Snowballs flying,
Children chanting,
'Snowball fight'
On the playground.

Children slipping,
Skating, skipping,
Sliding, gliding,
What a hullabaloo!

Jade Guest (10)
North Featherstone JI School

THE RUSH

Rushing in the morning,
Every single day,
Rushing in the evening,
Every single day.

Commotion in the living room,
Every single week,
Commotion in my bedroom,
Every single week.

Frantically panting,
Every single month,
Frantically puffing,
Every single month.

All together,
They make a bunch,
One, two and three.

Jo-Louise Knibb (11)
North Featherstone JI School

HULLABALOO!

Hullabaloo, hullabaloo
What's this entire hullabaloo?
Here, there and everywhere,
There's always hullabaloo.
Cars in a traffic jam,
Beeping horns, people not stopping,
Oh no, that was a gigantic bang!

In my bedroom it's a hullabaloo,
Can't find anything,
Oh, what a disorganised mess,
I can't even find my bin!

I hate this hullabaloo, it's such a pest,
I wish it would finish,
It does for me when I go to bed!

Amy Windmill (10)
North Featherstone JI School

HULLABALOO

Children racing around the place,
Snowballs hitting people in the face,
A slippy, slidy playground is fun all day through,
Our playground's a hullabaloo.

Children falling in a snowball fight,
What a chaotic hour it is,
Oops! Mrs Smith's been hit,
I only kicked a little bit,
'Who was that? Bethany, to the wall.'
Is it illegal to throw a snowball?
My play's over but that doesn't stop . . .
The hullabaloo!

Bethany Hiorns (11)
North Featherstone JI School

HULLABALOO!

The M25 is busy
It's a *hullabaloo!*
It is rush hour
Cars speed up and down
Turning and crashing
Breaking down
Petrol going down fast
Tyres going fast
Engines not working
It's a *hullabaloo!*

Jack Nicholson (8)
North Featherstone JI School

CORO'S HULLABALOO!

Karen nosy,
Kirk dozy,
Maxine's dead,
'Oh dear' said Fred.
Doreen's fifty,
Something's nifty.

Fizz sewing,
Gail not knowing,
Maxine's baby,
Ashley's maybe?
Nelson's lying,
Roy is frying.

Toyah's sad,
Norris is mad.
Ade accused,
Emily confused.
Todd fancies Sarah-Lou,
Oh what a hullabaloo!

Danielle Gale (11)
North Featherstone JI School

READY STEADY RUSH!

'Get a pan,'
Ainsley sang.
Potato in,
Carrots thin.
'10 minutes to go.'
Microwave on,
Mince long,
'No, that's wrong!'
Stir the soup,
Onion ring loop.
'5 minutes to go.'
Get the plates,
We're gonna be late!
Grab the food,
Put it on.
'Stop rushing!'
Phew, we're done!

Louise Garland-Jones (10)
North Featherstone JI School

HULLABALOO

Rushing, running, pushing, pulling, hurrying here and there.
Commotion, chaotic, this family does not care.
Frantic, fussing, why is everybody so mean?
This is a disaster, the biggest one I've seen.

Screaming, shouting, that's all these children do.
People saying, 'I never did like you.'
Crying, crawling, I hate this family tree.
Fighting, frustrated, they're nothing like me.

Rushing, running, pushing, pulling, hurrying here and there.
Commotion, chaotic, this family does not care.
Frantic, fussing, why is everybody so mean?
This is a disaster, the biggest one I've seen.

Abby Leach (11)
North Featherstone JI School

ICY HULLABALOO

Sliding, slipping, skidding,
Everyone on the floor,
People cry with laughter,
No one stands anymore.

Children, teachers, parents,
Having fun at break,
Laughing, shouting, crying,
What a racket they make.

All this fun must stop soon,
As all the children now knew,
Falling on ice really hurts,
When it's *hullabaloo!*

Sean Stones (11)
North Featherstone JI School

SNOWBALL FIGHT

Slipping and sliding on the twinkling ice
It's a hullabaloo
Take my advice
Chaos, commotion, duck for cover!
Everyone's tripping all over each other
In a frenzy of excitement
Scooping up snow
I hurl a snowball
At my brother
What a brilliant throw!
Covered in glittering powder
Dripping cold and wet
I squeal like a pig
A snowball fight
Has been set
Slipping and sliding on the twinkling ice
It's a hullabaloo, take my advice.

Amy Schofield (10)
North Featherstone JI School

HULLABALOO!

There are people rushing,
Screaming all around,
It's total chaos,
Just listening to the sound.

People running up and down the stairs,
Making banging that thumps through my head,
Every time I try to sleep,
There are people bouncing on my bed.

Nobody can ever stop,
Screaming, shouting, whatever, whenever,
It is total chaos,
But the people are my family
And I will love them forever.

Nichola Howarth (9)
North Featherstone JI School

AUTUMN LEAVES

The wind blew
And I was free.
I hovered in the air like a bird,
I swished and swirled;
With not a care in the world,
I felt dizzy,
I dived as the wind caught me,
I felt terror,
I landed gently,
In the middle of a new world,
My new friends laughed with glee,
Whilst I lived in fear of turning brown and crinkly.

Samuel Ian Parkinson (11)
Oyster Park Junior School

TURTLE SONG

Giant shell in the sea,
Turtle I heard you,
Grieving.

Dishes for women
And ashtrays for me.

Enormous creature in the ocean,
Crying for your life, crying for your kind,
Why are you dying?

Dishes for women
And ashtrays for men.

Bradley Thornton (9)
Oyster Park Junior School

AROUND THE CAULDRON GO

All the garbage from the bin,
In goes a fish's fin,
A fenny heart from a dog
And green skin peeled from a frog.

An intestine from a human being,
A slimy eye of a newt,
A tongue of a wild snake,
Which we baked in a cake.

A poisoned beak from a duck,
In the cauldron, boil and cook,
A tail of pig, a foot of bat,
An eye of cow and tongue of cat.
In the cauldron they go,
To be cooked, then to be eaten.

Chloe Beattie (10)
Oyster Park Junior School

HAIKUS

Haikus are poems
They go five, seven then five
With only three lines.

Marcus Dale (10)
Oyster Park Junior School

ANGRY

Angry is scarlet red.
It tastes like burning hot peppers.
It smells like a blazing fire.
It looks like balls of fire.
It sounds like alarms going off.
It feels like getting burnt by hot lava.

Ashleigh Carr (9)
Oyster Park Junior School

NEGLECT

Neglect is grey like six o'clock in the morning.
It tastes like raw onions.
It smells like burning wood.
It looks like a raging tornado tearing up my dreams.
It sounds like silence on a road full of cars.

Shanelle Bateman (10)
Oyster Park Junior School

NEGLECTED

Neglect is dull grey.
It tastes like cold chips.
It smells like rubber climbing up your nose.
It looks blank in your messed-up mind.
It sounds like a crashing heart.
It feels like a bullet through your mind.

Zarina Earnshaw (9)
Oyster Park Junior School

ROMANCE

Romance is blood-red.
It tastes like sugary strawberries and cream.
It smells like faint breezes of perfume.
It looks like a never-ending kiss.
It sounds like bluebirds chirping a love song.
It feels like a magical love spell.

Karin Ward (10)
Oyster Park Junior School

HATE

Hate is flaming red.
It tastes like *dark blood*.
It smells like a swamp.
It looks like a red devil.
It sounds like a steam train.
It feels like strength running in my body.

Jordan Palmer (10)
Oyster Park Junior School

FRIGHTENED

Frightened is red
It tastes like ice cubes on my tongue
It smells like rotten bodies
It looks like ghosts in a hall
It sounds like axes chopping
It feels like someone's breathing on the back of my neck.

Daniel Carter (10)
Oyster Park Junior School

THE VOLCANO

The volcano was a horrible, angry giant,
Shaking his enormous fists,
His voice banged like a drum on the hillside,
His thick black hair was smoky and luminous,
His eyes were red and full of destruction.

Jaime Blythe (11)
Oyster Park Junior School

THE VOLCANO

The volcano was an angry giant shaking its fists.
Its voice trembled through the town.
Its red hair covered the village!
Knotting together the roads and shops.
Its eyes blinked angrily with fury.

Terri-Leigh Woolford (11)
Oyster Park Junior School

In My Photo I Can See...

In my photo I can see
My sister and me,
The beaming light shining through the window,
Like a blazing fire starting to glow.
The luminous colours from all around,
Dazzling in the background.
My sister, smiling happily,
But not me.
I was staring nervously,
Why?
I cannot remember.
In my photo I can see
My sister and me.

Jade Blackburn (11)
Oyster Park Junior School

Autumn Leaves

I am a rusty colour now,
I am waiting for a big gust of wind to take me,
Shake me,
Free me,
So I can explore the waiting world.
To leave home
And travel through the sky.
I snap from the tree,
I flutter through the sky,
I glide through the air,
As I flutter like a bird
And dive to death.

Alice Carlyle (10)
Oyster Park Junior School

AN EXTRA VERSE FOR MACBETH

The second witch walked up to the cauldron,
Round about the cauldron go:
Dead dog's claws, live dog's heart;
Venom of a fenny cobra,
Earwax of a zebra.
Rattle of a slither snake, squash it in some chocolate cake.
Eye of eagle,
Beak of seagull,
Black widow's cauldron.
For the ingredients of our cauldron.

Leanne Kirby (11)
Oyster Park Junior School

AUTUMN LEAVES

I swiftly floated away from home
Proud of my radiant multicoloured skin
Blown away from my home
I felt regret
Sadness
At leaving everything that I knew
I landed by the damp riverside
I swayed away from my mother
As the sun burnt me to a crisp
I was brown and wrinkled
Like an old man's face
No more multicoloured skin
Brown and old.

Reanna Wallis (10)
Oyster Park Junior School

THE WRITER OF THIS POEM
(Based on 'The Writer Of This Poem' by Roger McGough)

The writer of this poem is . . .
As hard as a rock
As patterned as a butterfly
As strong as a door
As graceful as a pop star
As clumsy as an octopus
As harmless as a sea horse
As good a swimmer as an otter.
I am a?

Turtle.

Demi Davies (8)
Oyster Park Junior School

AUTUMN LEAF

I play with my friends,
Rolling wherever the gentle wind takes us.
Swooping,
Looking for new adventures,
Swirling through the air like birds,
I'm extremely brown.
No longer a bright polished green,
My body is wrinkled, I feel soggy and damp,
I feel dizzy,
I settle alone on the muddy floor,
To flutter, then die.

Jessica Strong (11)
Oyster Park Junior School

TURTLE SONG

Bumpy rock in the briny sea,
Turtle I heard you crying,
Your friends have been killed.

Ornaments for rich women,
Ashtrays for awful men.

Monstrous hill in the wavy ocean,
Turtle I hear you calling,
Calling for your friendship,
Why are you endangered?

Ornaments for rich women,
Ashtrays for awful men.

Wide mountain in the calm sea,
I feel your pain,
What's wrong with you?

Ornaments for rich women,
Ashtrays for awful men.

Ella Louise Spence (8)
Oyster Park Junior School

THE WRITER OF THIS POEM
(Based on 'The Writer Of This Poem' by Roger McGough)

The writer of this poem is . . .
As green as grass,
As hard as a rock,
As patterned as wrapping paper,
As strong as a wrestler,
As graceful as a clown,
As clumsy as a monkey,
As harmless as a baby,
As good a swimmer as a fish,
As wrinkly as a dress un-ironed,
As big as a house,
I am a?

Turtle.

Mandy Louise Armstrong (9)
Oyster Park Junior School

THE WRITER OF THIS POEM
(Based on 'The Writer Of This Poem' by Roger McGough)

The writer of this poem is . . .
As blue as the sky,
As graceful as a seal,
As cute as an otter,
As playful as a puppy,
As soft as a dog,
I am a?

Dolphin.

Zoe Brain (9)
Oyster Park Junior School

THE WRITER OF THIS POEM
(Based on 'The Writer Of This Poem' By Roger McGough)

The writer of this poem is . . .
As hard as a volcano,
As patterned as wallpaper,
As strong as scaffolding,
As graceful as a king,
As clumsy as a toddler,
As harmless as an ant,
As good at swimming as an otter,
As slow as a snail,
I am a?

Turtle.

Daniel Swift (9)
Oyster Park Junior School

THE WRITER OF THIS POEM
(Based on 'The Writer Of This Poem' By Roger McGough)

The writer of this poem is . . .
As hard as a rock,
As patterned as a picture,
As strong as a door,
As graceful as a starfish,
As clumsy as a cat,
As harmless as a dog,
As good a swimmer as a dolphin,
I am a?

Megan Noone (9)
Oyster Park Junior School

TURTLE SONG

Tiny hill in the calm sea
Turtle I heard you calling for your life

Soup and ashtrays for evil men
Ornaments for rich women
Turtle I heard you grieving for your life

Injured reptile in the sea
Caught in fishing nets
Turtle I heard you squealing for your kind

Turtle why are you dying?

Soup and ashtrays for evil men
Ornaments for rich women.

Becky Hand (9)
Oyster Park Junior School

TURTLE SONG

Turtle swimming in the tropical ocean,
Turtle I heard you singing.

Ashtrays for our rubbish,
Ornaments for our rooms.

Turtle grieving in the warm water,
Turtle I see you hunting.

Ashtrays for our rubbish,
Ornaments for our rooms.

Jade Barker (8)
Oyster Park Junior School

THE FOG

What was that?
Did you hear something?
The breeze and trees blended together
Like a silent orchestra
Rustle, rustle, rustle
The trees proceeding, proceeding towards me, murderously
I started to feel dizzy
A loud bellowing scream I let out
But who can stop me?
I'm fifty feet big with demonically huge teeth!
Who will I go for next?
Maybe you!

Kirsty Guthrie (9)
Oyster Park Junior School

TURTLE SONG

Turtle
You get hit by boats
And they don't care
Sport for evil men

Turtle
You get caught in fishing nets
And they don't care
Sport for evil men

Turtle
You can't lay eggs on busy beaches
They don't care
Sport for evil men.

Josh Birdsall (9)
Oyster Park Junior School

TURTLE SONG

Turtle
You are like a stepping stone,
In the wavy ocean,
Shells for ashtrays.

Turtle
You float through the warm water,
Searching for squid,
Shells for ashtrays.

Turtle
You search for empty beaches,
To lay your delicate eggs,
Shells for ashtrays.

Bethany Field (8)
Oyster Park Junior School

THE WRITER OF THIS POEM

(Based on 'The Writer Of This Poem' By Roger McGough)

The writer of this poem is . . .
As fat as a pancake,
He is as patterned as a mosaic,
He is as tall as a picture,

As slimy as a slug,
As crinkly as a trawl net,
As greedy as a pig,

His eyes are as sparkling as glitter,
As strong as a rock,
As clever as a monkey.

Ashley Yorke (8)
Oyster Park Junior School

MY PHOTO

In my photo I can see
Me as a baby with my make-up on me,
She must have known that I would destroy the make-up,
Well, that's just my mum.

She took a photo of me and showed my dad,
My mum laughed at me,
Well, that's just my mum.

The photo had been developed,
Everyone knew, not just one,
Well, that's just my mum.

Chelsea Jaine Land (11)
Oyster Park Junior School

I CAN STILL REMEMBER ...

I can still remember
When I had just broken up for the summer holidays
And you took a photo of me,
I put those owl-like glasses on,
Balancing on my ears and nose
And you took a photo of me,
I looked like an idiot,
I turned very red from head to toes
And you took a photo of me.

Ryan Smith (11)
Oyster Park Junior School

DO YOU REMEMBER WHEN I MOANED AND GROANED?

Do you remember when I moaned and groaned
When I walked down the street past sweets and ice cream
And the bright blue sea?

Rides passed in dashes
And children laughed with happiness
Then I moaned and groaned
When I walked down the street
It was a Saturday afternoon
And it was sticky and sunny

Then I moaned and groaned
As I walked down the street
Balloons went by
Seagulls screamed then
There I was laying as I sat on the ride.

Aran Starbuck (10)
Oyster Park Junior School

MEMORIES

Can you remember,
When I had my bike,
I sat on it and you took my photograph.

Can you remember,
It was in the morning,
It was a sunny morning,
I was smiling and you were laughing.

Can you remember,
I started peddling,
Like a circle going round and round.

Jessica Taylor (10)
Oyster Park Junior School

IN MY PHOTO

In my photo I can see
Me kicking a football
In the garden
With the family
The football is as round as a sphere
With a Nike tick on it
I scored a goal and shouted
The sun is golden
Just like shiny treasure
It lights the Earth
And a bird's colourful feather
The grass is green
The sky is blue
The ball is white
So different to the night.

Ryan Randle (10)
Oyster Park Junior School

CAN YOU REMEMBER WHEN?

Can you remember when
You soaked me with the hose pipe?
I had just got dressed into some dry clothes
I got really angry because I was very cold
Shivering, I turned to my mum, then the flash
The flash, the flash from a photo shone in my eyes
The photo was embarrassing
It was in the summer
The bright blue sky, no clouds, just blue sky.

Adam Rothwell (10)
Oyster Park Junior School

CAN YOU REMEMBER?

Can you remember the day when you picked me up
By my neck?
I didn't like it,
I hit you over the head.
Oh, I did,
Then you cried and Mum came in,
You said, 'Hayley hit me over the head.'
I said, 'Oh, I did,
Because you picked me up by my neck.'
You said, 'Why did you hit me over the head?'
I told you, 'You picked me up by my neck.'
Oh I did,
I hit you over the head.

Hayley Harling (10)
Oyster Park Junior School

IN THE BATH

I remember when
I was sitting in the bath one night
While my mum was watching with her sight
I was tempted to touch it with my hand
I tried to think of something else
Like sweets or chocolate or some pop
When just about to reach for the top
My mum shouts, 'Stop!'

Then it tempted me again
I tried to think of something else
Like sweets or chocolate or some pop
When just about to reach for the top
My mum shouts, 'Stop!'

Daniel Moore (11)
Oyster Park Junior School

AUTUMN LEAF

I'm hanging on my tree, proud of my lovely green colour,
Suddenly, the wind takes me in his strong arms.
I laugh gleefully as the wind tickles me with his thin fingers.
I laugh, roll around and play happily with my friends.
I am as free as a bird.
No one and nothing can tell me what to do.
I will explore the fields, the villages and cities,
The wind still holds tight to my stalk.
He takes me further and further away from my old home,
Old age slowly begins to creep up on me,
My colour begins to fade,
I feel like crying.
I begin to turn brown and orange,
My smooth pattern starts to disappear.
I'm becoming crispy and hard,
The wind finally lets me go.
I want to go home, back to my tree,
I gasp for air as I take my last breath,
My edges begin to crumble as I float to the hard ground,
I land in the mud.

Motionless and silent I lay down to rest . . .

Forever.

Kiera Whitworth (11)
Oyster Park Junior School

I REMEMBER

I remember when I was little,
I made an aeroplane out of pegs
And held it in the air and pointed it at real planes,
My dad took a picture,
I was little,
I stared into the sky with the model in my hand,
I was little.

Theresa Begley (11)
Oyster Park Junior School

VIKING

Vikings attacking the Saxon warriors,
Saxon warriors, Saxon warriors,
Vikings living in dingy huts,
Dingy huts, dingy huts,
Vikings attacking the evil sly king,
Evil sly king, evil sly king,
Vikings sailing out to sea,
Out to sea, out to sea.

Hanley Gaynor (7)
Ripponden JI School

PANCAKE DAY

It's as large as a mountain top!
It's as wide as a blue whale!
It's slishy, sloshy, slimy and greasy,
With lemon sauce and a cave of sugar
On top of the pancake!

Jonathan Porritt (8)
Ripponden JI School

CHRISTMAS DAY

Christmas tree, oh Christmas tree
Oh how I jump with glee

Lots of toys
Let's jump with joy

Mince pies
Santa cries
With whisky at his side

Children fast asleep
Come on, let's take a peep
Santa's fast asleep

Let's go now
I think Santa's waking

Next morning
I went to stop Dad from snoring
'Mum, Dad, it's Christmas Day.'

Isobel Wimbleton *(7)*
Ripponden JI School

CAN YOUR HEAR THE FIREWORKS?

Can you hear the fireworks
Banging all around?
Can you hear the fireworks
Zooming from the ground?
Can you hear the fireworks
Exploding in the air?
Can you hear the fireworks
Falling in despair?

Toby Rogers *(7)*
Ripponden JI School

CHRISTMAS, HO, HO, HO

C hildren playing around the Christmas tree
H olly and berries outside,
R obins flying in the air,
I cicles start to break,
S tockings hanging,
T insel on trees,
M istletoe on the windows,
A dvent calendars,
S anta's on his sleigh.

Ho, ho, ho, Merry Christmas.

Rebecca Callister (8)
Ripponden JI School

CHOCOLATE PUDDING

Chocolate pudding covered in sauce
Sauce rolling down and over the edge of the plate
Drip! Drip! Drip!
A chocolate mountain, soft and squidgy
With lots of tidgy chocolate chips, melting
It tastes soft, smooth, spongy, *yum!*

Ashley Campbell (8)
Ripponden JI School

CHRISTMAS

Christmas
Crackers
Cracking loudly,
Holly leaves
Green with berries
Red
Reindeer racing
Rudolph
Icicles sapping
In the snow
Sparkling tinsel
On the Christmas tree
Trees twinkling
With twinkling lights
Mince pies and mistletoe
Advent calendars
Lights bright in the church
Santa filling up stockings.

Charlotte Wolstenholme (7)
Ripponden JI School

SPLOEM

The splash splashed, splosh, splatter
Splonk, splurt, splice
Then split, splinter, splay, splinter, splonter
Splendour.

Meganne Green (8)
Ripponden JI School

A SPELL TO MAKE A RABBIT RED

Tomatoes hard, peppers red
Cranberries by the box, strawberries too

Red crayons, red shorts, red pens
Red jumpers, a basket
And a red shoe

Stir it well, stir it well
Abracadabra
A magic spell.

Jorja Nuttall *(8)*
Ripponden JI School

DOWN BEHIND THE DUSTBIN

Down behind the dustbin
I met a rat called Ratty
He ate loads of sweets
And he became a fatty

Then . . .

Down behind the dustbin
I met a lion called Hunter
I said, 'Why are you chewing my pencil?'
He said, 'To make it blunter.'

Connor Stephenson *(7)*
Ripponden JI School

CHRISTMAS

Christmas tree in the window,
Cold and shivery with nothing to eat,
Sitting in a doorway,
Cold night,
No mum and dad to care for me,
Help! Help! Please help!
No money to buy a sandwich,
Christmas has come,
Reindeer popping out of the sky
And someone in red, it is Santa.

Scott Sutcliffe *(7)*
Ripponden JI School

A SPELL TO MAKE A MONSTER

Drop it in, drop it in,
A toad, a spider, a bar of soap
A cricket black, four eyeballs green,
Drop it in, drop it in,
Two toenails from Frankenstein's feet,
Swamp mud brown, a mouse's ear,
Drop it in, drop it in,
Stir it well and make a spell.

Perry Stephen *(8)*
Ripponden JI School

THE BLACK RIDER

He comes with his powerful steed,
From the Dark Lord's black gate,
His giant claw made of iron and rust,
He comes from the western state.

He is mysterious with a cloak pulled over his head,
With a cloak pulled over his back.

The eye of Sauron is controlling Middle earth,
But this unknown rider rides at the dead of night,
He will wait and wait,
For the ring is almost in sight.

He is mysterious with a cloak pulled over his head,
With a cloak pulled over his back.

His horse is black with blood on the end of his foot,
But he groans with pain for he is weary, weary, weary,
This rider will not fail with his almost completed task,
The ring to the Rider is endearing, endearing, endearing.

He is mysterious with a cloak pulled over his head,
With a cloak pulled over his back.

Half dead, half living, he will find the ring,
He rides and rides and will kill the bearer,
His black cloak and face is frightful in the dark,
Who is this? This is the Black Rider.

Jack Johnstone (9)
St Andrew's Junior School, Brighouse

THE POEM OF THE BLACK RIDER

Searching on a dreadful steed
The cold-hearted rider as dull as death
Galloping at a frightful speed
Looking with all his greed

'Twas a silent windy night
Clear as clear can be
Lit by a moonlit light
Until the evil strike

His cloak as black as dust
His sinful face is hidden
No soul must he trust
And shows no mercy given

He can sense the ring's cruel curse
Screams and cries make his path
What beast could be any worse?
His power will stab any innocent heart.

Eva Khan (10)
St Andrew's Junior School, Brighouse

THE BLACK RIDER

The frightful Black Rider galloped across the forest
He's sensing, sensing, sensing,
He's going across the forest and he's sensing, sensing, sensing,
He's trying to find the ring to bring it to his master,
He's trying to find the ring on his black steed,
He's trying to find the ring to bring it to his master,
He's trying to find the ring on his black steed,
The forest is so dark that it would scare you out of your skin.

Gareth Hopkins (9)
St Andrew's Junior School, Brighouse

PRECIOUS

His name is Sméagol\Gollum
A Hobbit from by the river,
When he was young, good, he was not a taker but a giver.

He had a best friend who found a ring,
A very precious ring, it drove him mad this precious thing,
He killed his best friend for the ring.

He took it deep into the mountain for five hundred years
His life kept counting,
Then one day as time did linger,
The ring escaped from his finger.

Something happened, the ring did not intend,
It was found by Bilbo from Bag End.

Gollum screamed, shouted and hissed
Desperate for the precious thing he missed,
Slowly time passed in the gloom,
He heard of the ring going to the crack of doom.

So he followed Frodo and Sam,
Hoping to slaughter them like a lamb.
For months he travelled in disguise,
Telling Sam and Frodo lies.
Soon he senses the ring's time has come,
He couldn't dream of living without the one.

In a fit of rage he shouted, 'Liar!'
He bit off the finger of Frodo from the Shire.

At the edge of doom he toppled and fell,
Sméagol and his precious ring fell into the fires of Hell.

Chloe Kitcher (10)
St Andrew's Junior School, Brighouse

THE BLACK RIDER

The leaves were swirling round and round
Making an almighty sound
There the Black Rider stood
Covering his face with his long black hood
His huge, horrible horse gave a scream
Frodo wished this was a terrible dream

The Black Rider was riding, riding
On his huge, horrible horse
He could sense it, he could not see
Getting that ring was his destiny

His metal hand made a fist
He then fled off in a gloomy mist.

Emily Johnson (9)
St Andrew's Junior School, Brighouse

THE SOUND COLLECTOR
(Based on 'The Sound Collector' by Roger McGough)

A stranger called this morning
Dressed all in black and grey
Put every sound into a bag
And carried them away

The voices of the teachers
The ringing of the bell
The rustling of the paper
And even the people outside could tell

The scraping of school pencils
The turning of the lock
The whistling of the kettle
And the ticking of a clock.

Sarah Drake (10)
St Andrew's Junior School, Brighouse

THE SOUND COLLECTOR
(Based on 'The Sound Collector' by Roger McGough)

A stranger called this morning
Dressed all in black and grey
Put every sound into a bag
And carried them away

The scraping of the pencils
The stamping on the floor
The ringing of the school bell
The banging on a door

The talking of the children
The clashing of the bins
The yapping of the teachers
The chiming of the pins

The whistle of the cleaner
The whizzing of the vac
The rustle of the papers
The zipping of the sack

The clattering of the drawers
The dripping of the tap
The squeaking of the white chalk
The swishing of the map

A stranger called this morning
He didn't leave his name
Left us all only silence
Life will never be the same.

Annabel Wilson (9)
St Andrew's Junior School, Brighouse

THE BLACK RIDER

Through the swirly misty fog,
Galloping over a muddy bog.
The black hooded rider came into view,
He was here to snatch the ring that's what he must do.

The Black Rider is galloping, galloping, galloping,
The Black Rider is galloping to find the magical ring.

The light disappeared, the sun was gone,
The time of dark had just begun,
The Black Rider's face was dead and dusty,
The black cold armour was cold and rusty.

The trees began to whisper, whisper, whisper,
The trees began to whisper as the horse came to a halt.

The rider dismounted off his horrible horse,
He could sense the ring with his powerful force,
With his cold, hungry eyes jerking to and fro,
He remembered the death time many years ago.

He still keeps searching, searching, searching,
He still keeps searching to find his precious ring.

Amelia Thurlow (9)
St Andrew's Junior School, Brighouse

THE BLACK RIDER

The ring gets nearer, nearer and nearer.
He is getting closer, closer and closer.
He is nearly there.
He jumps off his horrible, haunted horse
To see if the rarest ring was there.

But all he could see was a misty atmosphere
With the dull, grey sky
And the racing river going by.
He gallops past the spooky wood,
Fluttering behind him was his black hood,
He thought he looked very good,
He can sense the ring,
He gallops as fast as he can.

The ring gets nearer, nearer and nearer,
He is getting closer, closer and closer.
He is nearly there.
He jumps off his horrible haunted horse
To see if the rarest ring was there.

It was there, the golden ring,
The rarest ring on the top of the hill,
Now he is the most powerful man of all.

Elise Marsden (9)
St Andrew's Junior School, Brighouse

THE SOUND COLLECTOR

(Based on 'The Sound Collector' by Roger McGough)

A stranger called this morning
Dressed all in black and grey
Put every sound into a bag
And carried them away

The banging of the instruments
The banging of the drum
The whistling of the whistle
The sound of the big hum

The singing of the choir
The ringing of the phone
The banging of the loud drum
That made the man go home

A stranger called this morning
He didn't leave his name
Left us only silence
Life will never be the same.

Stephen Hughes (9)
St Andrew's Junior School, Brighouse

THE BLACK RIDER

The image of the Black Rider was frightful,
As he came stealthily along the road,
Searching for the ring was his only thought.

The Black Rider came searching, searching,
The Black Rider came searching, searching,
He had to find the ring.

As the Black Rider came riding through the misty trees,
As the Black Rider came riding through the gloomy breeze.

The Black Rider came searching, searching,
The Black Rider came searching,
He had to find the ring.

There was darkness all around,
But up in the sky was a misty moon
Which hung over the rustling trees,
But in the forest there was nothing but gloom.

The Black Rider came searching, searching,
The Black Rider came searching, searching,
He had to find the ring.

Georgina Graham (9)
St Andrew's Junior School, Brighouse

THE BLACK RIDER

Through the very dense fog
The horse jumped over a broken log

The rough raging river
The rough raging river

The leaves blew around and around
And all lifted off the ground

He still keeps riding, riding, riding,
He still keeps riding to find the powerful ring

All the armour was very rusty
And it was all very dusty

The wild whistling wind
The wild whistling wind

The atmosphere was changing
And all was rearranging

He still keeps riding, riding, riding
He still keeps riding to find the powerful ring.

Lauren O'Brien (10)
St Andrew's Junior School, Brighouse

THE BLACK RIDER

The Black Rider came riding, riding, riding,
The Black Rider came riding to capture the powerful ring.

The fragile, freaky forest was hardly staying still,
If you go near the forest you easily could be ill.
The wild, whistling wind was breezy in the air,
He'd get you if you stand and stare.

The Black Rider came riding, riding, riding,
The Black Rider came riding to capture the powerful ring.

His long black cloak was covering his head,
Go near the Black Rider, you'll be dead!
If you look up very high,
You'll see the cloudy misty sky.

The Black Rider came riding, riding, riding,
The Black Rider came riding to capture the powerful ring.

The horrible horse hooves were riding in the smoke,
Everywhere you looked there weren't any folk.
It was like a ghostly galleon, a very windy breeze,
Nothing was still, not even the trees.

The Black Rider came riding, riding, riding,
The Black Rider came riding to capture the powerful ring.

Rachel Hunt (10)
St Andrew's Junior School, Brighouse

THE BLACK RIDER

The Black Rider came riding, riding, riding
The Black Rider came riding to the old, wooden trees
On his noble steed
He approached slowly towards the trees
And he is scary
He is strong when he is angry
He wears black baggy clothes
The trees were blowing strongly
The owls were hunting
The sky was moving towards the trees
Silence strikes when he approaches.

Emily Beth Parkinson (9)
St Andrew's Junior School, Brighouse

THE BLACK RIDER

The Black Rider came riding, riding, riding
The Black Rider came riding to try to find the ring
Watching the road twist and turn around
And listening to this awful sound
Listening to the calm, calm breeze
As it reaches up to the tall, tall trees
The Black Rider came riding, riding, riding
The Black Rider came riding to try to find the ring
Watching the calm, trickling river
Look at him, he'll make you quiver
Screaming, screeches in your ears
Will bring you up to your horrible fears
The Black Rider came riding, riding, riding
The Black Rider came riding to try to find the ring.

Faith Thewlis (10)
St Andrew's Junior School, Brighouse

THE BLACK RIDER

In the dark forest the horse was chomping,
As they went on to find the ring,
The horse was chomping and started stomping,
The Black Rider could sense the ring.

The Black Rider was riding, riding, riding through the wind.

The Black Rider was riding in the mist,
Determined to find the ring,
The horse wanted to twist,
Suddenly the Black Rider nearly caught the ring.

The Black Rider was riding, riding through the mist.

The ring was really glowing,
In the misty forest,
The Black Rider was riding as he came flowing,
Over the golden ring.

Natasha Smith (10)
St Andrew's Junior School, Brighouse

THE BLACK RIDER

As the Black Rider came cantering through the monstrous forest fog
On his big black stallion
He stopped for a moment or two
And felt a particular breeze coming off the trees
Just then his long black cloak was telling him something
You're getting nearer, nearer
You're getting nearer to the gold ring
He stopped and shuffled his head side to side on the huge cold road
His thick black cloak slyly emerged
Like a thick cheetah that had pounced on its prey
And the trees looked like monstrous thieves.

Rebecca Howard (9)
St Andrew's Junior School, Brighouse

KIRK

Kirk, cute and small,
Plays with a ball,
High on yells,
Better than six alarm bells,
Calls for his mummy,
To fill his tummy,
Kirk couldn't burst a bubble,
Honest he's never in trouble.

God bless, it's time for bed,
Time to rest your sleepy head,
God bless, sweet dreams,
The night is never what it seems,
God bless, all locked up,
Where it is safe and all you see is a smiling face,
God bless, all through the night,
Without a peep,
Then morning comes, no more time for sleep.

Gemma Melhuish (10)
St Clare's RC Primary School, Bradford

IN THE JUNGLE

In the jungle many animals lurk,
Sometimes it's hot and sometimes it's cold,
Monkeys swing from tree to tree,
Hippopotami swim in the river
While elephants have their tea
But the king of the jungle
Roars!

Lauren Hickey (8)
St Clare's RC Primary School, Bradford

ANIMAL ALPHABET

A   is for antelope which fleets through the plains,
B   is for bear who has suffered a lot of pain,
C   is for a chameleon with a very special skin,
D   is for donkey who's just kicked someone's shin,
E   is for elephant with a huge, grey trunk,
F   is for frog who can really, really jump,
G   is for giraffe with a long, tall neck,
H   is for horse with a brown and white check,
I   is for iguana with its long green tail,
J   is for jackal who won't fail,
K   is for kangaroo with a joey in its pouch,
L   is for lemur who likes a good slouch,
M   is for meerkat who stands up tall,
N   is for narwhal who has a beautiful call,
O   is for ostrich with gigantic eggs,
P   is for pony with chunky little legs,
Q   is for quails with small, chubby heads,
R   is for rabbit with a chewy mint peg,
S   is for seal which swims so gracefully,
T   is for turtle who relaxes in the sea,
U   is for urchin which sticks to the rocks,
V   is for viper with a skin like colourful blocks,
W   is for wolf with a beautiful face,
X   is for unknown, so don't get on my case,
Y   is for yak with a huge back,
Z   is for zebra which are stalked by a lion pack.

Gabrielle Crabtree (10)
St Clare's RC Primary School, Bradford

ABUSED CHILD

I know that we're short of money
And I know that I'm not very bright.
But why do you always beat me?
Is it just to give me a fright?

I know that you must be angry
And I know that you try your best.
But beating me won't help at all -
Can't you just give it a rest?

I know it's been hard since Mum died,
But Dad, it's been hard for me too.
I've had to put up with dry bread
And bottles of Irn-Bru.

I know it's all we can afford, Dad,
But I want a little bit more.
It doesn't cost any money,
Is love too much to ask for?

Mary-Clare Newsham (10)
St Clare's RC Primary School, Bradford

ANIMALS

Cats are furry,
Cute and scary,
Dogs move fast
And are never last.
Rabbits have soft, warm fur,
Which matches their fluffy tails,
Wolves howl, scratch and scowl,
See, animals aren't so bad after all!

Jane Nicholson (10)
St Clare's RC Primary School, Bradford

THE TROUBLE WITH BABIES

Babies are so cute, they're as pretty as fruit,
Oh no, I'm joking, I'm telling you a lie;
Babies are not as sweet as a cherry or apple pie,
Babies are little brats,
They are in your shoes, they are in your hats,
They do not like taking a bath,
Also they have an awful crooked laugh.
They like to eat yoghurts and Sunday lunch,
They pull flowers out of the bunch.
They spit out their dummy -
They think this is funny.
But now I'll have to see,
Just what the stork will bring for me.

Alice Jukes (10)
St Clare's RC Primary School, Bradford

FOOTBALL!

As the football is in the air
Man United is on the air
And feeling scared!

Leeds are learning
United are burning
The score is three-nil

Leeds are short-sighted
So are United
But the winners are delighted.

Daniel Parkinson (9)
St Clare's RC Primary School, Bradford

148

MY PUPPY

Puppies need lots of care
Even when they're on the stair
Drinking water - *slurp, slurp, slurp*
Watch out - here comes a great big burp!
Digging holes in the flower bed
'Oh no! My flowers,' my poor mum said.

Out for walks, fun in the park
Oh no! Another dog! *Bark, bark, bark!*
In the bath, *splash, splash, splish*
Looking in the tank at the colourful fish

Chewing toys, clothes, balls
'Oh silly dog!' my dad calls
Brushing her coat, making it shine
I love my puppy, she's mine, all mine
Ears flapping in the breeze
I grab her ball and my puppy I tease

Eating food, greedy as can be
Oh no! She's done a wee!
Snoozing in her cosy bed
Crawling under the table, puppy watch your head
My puppy likes playing around everywhere
My puppy needs a great deal of care.

Emma Croot (11)
St Clare's RC Primary School, Bradford

CELEBRITY

Roll out the carpet, red if you please,
Then get ready to fall to your knees
And call out, 'Autographs please.'

Flash, flash, click, click,
Hurry up, best be quick
And in your excitement don't be sick.

They never look ugly, they try to dress nice,
Even when it's cold as ice.

Glamour and glitz,
Tantrums and fits,
A stay at the Ritz,
Posh houses, fast cars,
How we like to look up to the stars

Films, theatres, premieres,
Even boring village fairs,
LA, London, Hollywood,
I would be one if I could.

We know the names of all the stars,
Posh and Becks, Gareth and Will,
They all like to give us a thrill.

What would life be
Without a celebrity?

Thomas Lock (9)
St Clare's RC Primary School, Bradford

MY TWO SISTERS

In this poem you will find,
That my two sisters can be silly and kind.
My eldest sister is snazzy and trendy,
The other is noisy, chatty and friendly.

My little sister likes to play with me,
She also likes to watch my TV,
Quite a lot she will moan and weep,
At bedtime she won't go to sleep.

My biggest sister goes on her mobile phone,
She often likes to be left alone.
Sometimes on her door I knock,
She calls out, 'Dad! I need a lock!'

My younger sister chats with her dolls,
She says they're alive and takes them on her hols.
She doesn't like to eat her tea,
She says, 'I don't want it unless you feed me.'

My older sister's room is where she stays,
She says she doesn't want to play.
She's too busy to talk to me unless,
I ask her a question and it's 'No' or 'Yes'.

I'm in the middle of these two pests,
They're completely opposite as you have guessed.
Sometimes I think, why can't it be
Why can't my sisters be more like me?

Eleanor Willis (11)
St Clare's RC Primary School, Bradford

MY FAMILY

Mum, Dad, Charlotte and me,
Makes up my family,
Our auntie Linda, uncle Andrew,
Becky, Jonathan, Alex and Sam
Are a part of our family.

Our grandma Rhodes has a funny cat,
That likes playing with wool,
I usually play with her,
We play with a skipping rope.

Our grandma Mitchell likes
Giving us treats
And buying all sorts of things;
Sometimes she gives us a ten pound note!

Mummy, Daddy, Charlotte and me,
Make up our family,
We love each other very much,
Even when we scream and shout,
That's why we are one big happy family!

Catherine Mitchell (7)
St Hilda's School, Wakefield

ANIMALS

In this world we have animals,
All kinds of mammals
And others too,
All for you.

The tiger is king,
His roar is an enormous ring,
As he prowls along,
He growls.

The turtle is my pet,
I hate it when he gets all wet,
He wins every race,
At his own steady pace.

The dove is snowy-white,
High, high is her flight,
It is her right,
To take a very big flight.

Jodie Burnley (8)
St Hilda's School, Wakefield

THE SNAKE

The snake is called Sam,
He's a poisonous one,
He's shiny and slippery
And not much fun.

His body is long,
He wriggles and moves,
His tongue is pointy,
He hides in grooves.

Emily Lodge (7)
St Hilda's School, Wakefield

MY KITTEN, WHITE-SOCKS

My kitten, White-Socks is very playful,
She likes to make my knitting knotty,
I often find her climbing everywhere,
She plays all day without a care.

My kitten, White-Socks has black glossy fur,
Her paws are snow-white,
Her eyes are emerald-green,
She is the most handsome kitten,
I have ever seen.

My kitten, White-Socks is special to me,
I like to give her treats,
She sits on my lap for hours on end,
And there's no doubt she's my best friend.

Eleanor Newton (8)
St Hilda's School, Wakefield

THE SKY AT NIGHT

The moon is wonderful,
Shining like a disco ball,
Gleaming very white;
In the black of night,
It shines against the stars,
It gleams really bright.

The moon shines really bright,
Against the starry night;
Sometimes it has a full face,
Sometimes it has a crescent shape.

Amber Johnson (8)
St Hilda's School, Wakefield

MY BIRTHDAY

I am having a party,
With a cake all covered in Smarties.
All my friends are coming,
With different gifts and presents,
In brightly-coloured paper,
Big ones, small ones, large ones,
Every kind of size and colour!

We will have some party music
And play the party games,
Pass the parcel and blind man's buff.
My cake will have nine candles . . .
A pink one, blue one, every kind of size and colour,
I am with my friends, we will laugh and have fun,
As it's my birthday, I'm the special one!

My mum organised my party,
It has been great,
Though I'm a bit sad, I'm no longer eight,
I am one year older,
I am now nine,
It's exciting to get bigger,
I'm growing all the time!

Harriet Willings (8)
St Hilda's School, Wakefield

MY GRANDMA

Grandma, Grandma, Grandma,
I love it at Grandma's,
On Friday nights I stay at Grandma's,
I eat KFC,
Grandad has spicy chicken and chapatti,
When we're finished, I help Grandma clean the dishes,
Just before we go to bed.

Grandma is kind,
Grandma plays with me,
Grandma takes me swimming,
She jumps in and does a belly flop,
Which is very funny!

Grandma can sometimes be quite moody,
But when she laughs, her face lights up,
When she's cross her face turns beetroot-pink,
She can shout but when she mellows,
She's still so funny,
My grandma,
I love her just the same.

Rhea Patel (8)
St Hilda's School, Wakefield

MY CUTE FRIENDLY KITTEN

I have a kitten,
It is black and white,
With round, brown eyes and a big black nose,
Its cheeky sly smile,
Makes me happy.

Its furry fluffy fur,
Feels all cuddly,
It miaows, miaows softly
And is sly and very cheeky,
When it rolls in mud,
It comes home dirty.

When I stroke my cute friendly kitten,
It purrs for me gently,
Like a little baby
And makes me feel warm inside.

Sehrish Butt (8)
St Hilda's School, Wakefield

ANGRY WORDS

Angry words are like spiky pins stabbing through me
Angry words are like hard stones flung in your face
Angry words are like round balls thrown at you
Angry words are like sharp scissors cutting through your heart
Angry words are like a nail being stabbed into your head
Angry words are like sparkling lightning striking you.

Melissa Doyles (8)
St Hilda's School, Wakefield

MY FAMILY

My mum has gleaming rings
That sparkle through the night,
The sight of them are shining bright,
All day and all night.

My dad who likes cars,
Also works hard,
He works all night
And is very bright.

My sister called Lily
Is very, very silly,
She has curly hair
And does not want to share.

Nanan Pauline eats very healthy,
Maybe one day she might be wealthy,
She is very sweet and kind
And she's all mine.

Grandad Major is very clever,
He reads the news and watches the weather,
He cleans his cars all day and night,
Until they sparkle very bright.

Nanan Kath she likes to bake,
Lots of buns and chocolate cake,
She's very old but very dear
And she lives very near.

That's my family all summed up,
I love them all so very much.

Chloe Sunderland (7)
St Hilda's School, Wakefield

GIRAFFES

Giraffes have big necks to eat leaves and fruits,
Giraffes have long legs to run with,
Giraffes have yellow and orange patches,
Giraffes live in hot countries like South Africa and America.

Giraffes run and walk in the zoo,
Giraffes eat big bunches of branches when they are hungry,
Giraffes can see from miles away,
Tell me giraffe, what can you see from miles away?

Do you giraffes see lots of trees?
Baby giraffes, do you nibble lots of food?
Giraffes, do you see as far as the clouds?
Giraffes, you are lucky to have those very long legs
Which help you to run so fast.

Holli Yu (7)
St Hilda's School, Wakefield

MY NANNY

Nanny you are so beautiful, your face is like a rose
Your lips glisten in the dark, oh I love you so

When you come to stay,
You make a little noise that makes me feel so special inside
And whenever I feel upset or angry
I think of you and your special sound.

When you knit and sew I watch you very carefully,
You are a special person, of this I know it's true,
I ring you up, you smile at me
And then I'm never blue.

Jade Wolfenden (8)
St Hilda's School, Wakefield

WHEN I GO TO BED

When I go to bed
Dad says, 'Rest your sleepy head'
I toss and turn and wriggle around
Until it is time to snuggle down

Sheep appear in my head
Are they really at the bottom of my bed?
They jump around and bleat
And nibble at my feet

I'm sleepy now
It's very dark
Into dreamland now I go
Counting sheep
To get to sleep
Until tomorrow
See you then
At seven am
Goodnight sleepyhead!

Hayleigh Edson *(8)*
St Hilda's School, Wakefield

MY FIRST TIME AT MAJORETTES

A majorette I wanted to be
My mummy said she would take me
It was Wednesday night
The church hall was in sight

I had butterflies in my tummy
I really just wanted my mummy
I heard the music start
I could hear my heart . . .

I was dancing and all the horrible feelings were gone
I danced and sang along
The batons twirled
The pom-poms whirled

I have been going for quite a while
And it always brings a happy smile
I like the shows
They bring a tinkle to my toes.

Natalie English (8)
St Hilda's School, Wakefield

SUPERSONIC SNAIL

I've got a pet snail,
That I keep in a cage,
He's really and truly,
The best that's ever made.

He's as fit as a fiddle,
As strong as an ox
And he practices press-ups
Each day in his box.

He holds the world record
For running a metre,
It took him a week,
But he's still a world beater!

Bethany Johnson (9)
St Hilda's School, Wakefield

UNDERWATER TRAFFIC

Deep beneath the ocean floor
The big blue whale blows its horn
Beep beep!
The starfish shout from all about
And try to go through red!
The sharks they sneak across the street
Causing mayhem everywhere
So now you know it's true
The seas are really alive!

Emma Grainger (10)
St Mary's CE Primary School, Boston Spa

HULLABALOO

H ulla, hullabaloo
U pside down umbrellas
L ights flashing on and off
L eaves swirling all around
A ccidents waiting to happen
B lustering winds howling
A ngry skies above
L ightning flashing down
O ver and over bins tumble
O h what a hullabaloo.

Grace Barrett (8)
St Mary's CE Primary School, Boston Spa

HULLABALOO

H ullabaloo, what a hullabaloo
U pturned umbrellas everywhere
L eaves swooping, people stare
L adders falling, my dad glares
A bove the rooftops, losing your cares
B alls bouncing up the stairs
A nimals stampeding, teeth bared
L opsided dustbins, wind blowing my hair
O ops! I forgot to put my shoes in pairs
O h what a hullabaloo!

Naomi Barrow (8)
St Mary's CE Primary School, Boston Spa

THE WEATHERMAKER

Lightning in his eye
A hurricane in his hand
Storms in his spine
He can even make weather
That's really fine

The day demons descend
From the sun
The night nymphs emerge
From the river
And together they play
In the twilight
While the weathermaker watches
From his high, high tower
Watches
Watches
Watches.

Liam Livesley (8)
St Mary's CE Primary School, Boston Spa

SPRING

Getting lighter
Fields brighter
Days longer
Peddle-pushers shorter
Flowers blooming
Lambs skipping
Breeze warming
Perfect camping
It's spring.

Polly Whitelam (8)
St Mary's CE Primary School, Boston Spa

BUGS

Big bugs,
Tall bugs,
Bowling down the alley bugs.

Small bugs,
Slow bugs,
Diving in the loo bugs.

Fast bugs,
Flying bugs,
Dancing on the stage bugs.

Mad bugs,
Bad bugs,
Sleeping in your bed bugs.

Old bugs,
New bugs,
Hiding out of view bugs.

Lazy bugs,
Crazy bugs,
Buzzing round your ear bugs.

Buzzzzz.

Laura Pattison (9)
St Mary's CE Primary School, Boston Spa

THE CAT

I admired the ears, three cheers
I admired the claws, applause
And if somebody caught a rat
And squashed my black hat, it wasn't me.
I admired your tail, but don't let it get stuck in the mail.
I admired your smile, worthwhile
And if somebody climbed up the tree
And scratched my neighbour's knee, it wasn't me.
I admired your sleep, *beep beep*,
I admired your eyes, surprise
And if somebody went outside and caught a bird and it died,
It wasn't me
And if somebody sat on my bed and scratched my favourite ted,
It wasn't me.
I admired the fur, well durr.
I admired your purr as you were
And if somebody climbed the wall and pretended to be very small
And if somebody knocked over my light and had a fight with the kite,
It wasn't me.

Jessica Coates (9)
St Mary's CE Primary School, Boston Spa

DRAGON

In a cave, dark and wide
Is the place where I will hide
Till the sun is set on top of a hill
Is the time when I will kill
Who am I?

I breathe fire that is hot
To make people freeze right to the spot
My colour is blazing red
And I have a very big head
What am I?

I am a dragon
My name rhymes with wagon
I am very hungry, so what will I do?
I am coming to eat all of you!

Natalie Heaton (9)
St Mary's CE Primary School, Boston Spa

FAIRIES LURKING IN THE GARDEN

Fairies are in the garden
Collecting hidden treasures for their warm cosy homes
Little acorn cases for their cups
And birds' feathers for their quilts
Rainbowdrop, one of the queen fairies
Collecting rose petals for the secret ball
Starburst collecting dew to use as champagne
Fairies fluttering from tree to tree
Making sure that nobody sees them!

Naomi Allan (10)
St Mary's CE Primary School, Boston Spa

FUSSY PUSSY

I'm a fussy pussy
A Clifford cat
When it comes to food
I like *rat!*
My name is Oscar
I live down the lane
Every dude in Clifford
Knows my name
There's a new dog in the house
I can't get in
So I eat the mouse!
Her name is Ellie
She smells like a welly
When she's in the car
She slobbers like jelly!
When she sees me
She thinks *hey cat!*
She gets so excited
She wees on the mat!
She's got a friend
Her name is Miss Bean
She's actually a Jack
But she thinks she's the Queen!
When she goes out, she needs a coat
And when it rains, she tries to float
Her legs are so small
She could do with a boat
Us three pets in the house
Have a midnight feast
What do we want? We want a mouse.

Holly Bonelle (10)
St Mary's CE Primary School, Boston Spa

168

MISS UNDERSTOOD

Some people say that she's no good
She's really just too wild
But when willing parents come round
She pretends she's a really good child

Her enemy, Jade, read her story
Saying it was a disaster
But how she cried
When her nose was covered in plaster

She's up for any kind of dare
Really she'll do anything -
Once she ate five worms
And they were wriggling!

Grace Lindsey (9)
St Matthew's RC Primary School, Bradford

MY BROTHER

My brother is silly,
He jumps on you when he's happy,
But I have to agree,
He is a fast runner,
He makes me laugh when I'm sad
And plays with me when I'm lonely,
It's good to have a brother because
He's there with you all your life.

Kieran Lad (10)
St Matthew's RC Primary School, Bradford

THE DANCING WOLF

Today I saw a dancing wolf
In the park, a day in June
A man standing there
A whip in his hands

All the children came
All laughing at
The poor dancing wolf

The keeper shouted, 'Dance quick or be whipped'
The wolf started to dance more quickly
The keeper started to whip him because
He slowed down
He did not notice that the wolf did not want to dance

One paw up
One paw down
The poor wolf dancing

Then suddenly the laughter stopped
The old man came with a begging cup

They all gave money just for the show
But in the wolf's eyes were
Forests and the cold place where
He wants to be.

Sophie Priestley (10)
St Matthew's RC Primary School, Bradford

MY ROOM

In my room there's smelly socks,
There's old jigsaws and old toy blocks.

Under my bed,
There's a Barbie's head.

'Help your sister tidy her room,
Until it's as clean as a dot!'

'No thanks, Mum,
I'd rather not!'

That's what my brother would say,
Why didn't he help me
On that fine playing out day?

Rebecca Wilson (11)
St Matthew's RC Primary School, Bradford

MONSTER IN THE CUPBOARD

There's a monster in the cupboard
Oh no, what shall I do?
I know - I'll hide in the loo
I'll just have a look
Hey, his hand is a hook!
Maybe I'll shout my mum
Better not, she might smack my bum
There's a monster in the cupboard
Argh!

Dean Armitage (11)
St Matthew's RC Primary School, Bradford

ALL MY DREAMS AND THOUGHTS

All my dreams and thoughts are made there,
While I sit and have a good stare.

Maybe I want a swimming pool
Or a hotel in Blackpool.

One day I might have a castle,
Lay on pillows that have frilly tassels.

I dream of holidays far away,
Exotic countries where I might stay.

What would I look like in that purple flowing gown?
Would people think I looked like a clown?

I'd like to be a superstar
And drive around in a big flash car.

Then I'd come back from space,
I'd look around and I'd be in my own place.

Bethany Taylor (11)
St Matthew's RC Primary School, Bradford

THE HUNGRY DRAGON

He lives in the mountains;
He lurks behind the rocks;
He drinks at the fountain;
He eats lots and lots.
The things he eats are goats
And mountain lions too,
But watch out, his favourite food is
You!

Riccardo Coppola (11)
St Matthew's RC Primary School, Bradford

THE MACHINE

Last year I got a present,
A very big present,
With knobs and cogs,
That hummed loudly.

I pulled a lever,
Then flicked a switch
And then just
Pressed the *on* switch.

It jerked and rattled
And violently shook
And caused the room
To gleam with light.

The cogs still hummed
And engines rattled,
Wheels still turned
And pistons moved.

The room still gleamed like
A star in the night
And we gave the
Neighbours such a fright.

One angry neighbour
Hammered on the door,
*'Turn that thing off
Or I'll break down the door!'*

I again pulled a lever
And flicked a switch
And pressed the *off* switch.

Alex Conlon (9)
St Matthew's RC Primary School, Bradford

THE MADHATTER

Ian rides through the night
And in the morning the sun is bright,
Ian finally rides back to town
And sees Tony as a clown,
Ian asks, 'What's the matter?'
This is the work of the madhatter.

Ian goes to the madhatter's house,
But all he sees is *Micky Mouse*,
Micky Mouse is going to the beach,
But all he sees is James And The Giant Peach

The peach explodes and James says, 'Oh dear!'
Then they see a reindeer,
In its mouth is the key,
That will set Ian free.

He got the key, took it back,
Put his coat on the rack,
Opened the door, got the chest
And the madhatter was under arrest!

Thomas Stokes (10)
St Matthew's RC Primary School, Bradford

WHAT'S IN THE STAFFROOM?

'Get your shoes on quick,
Don't you want a break?
Cos I've got to go to the staffroom.'

'What's in there, Miss Gillon?
Is it icky tea and coffee?
Is that what's in the staffroom?'

'No, it's a luxury room!
With Liquorice Allsorts and Sky TV!
That's what we want to be in the staffroom,' they say.

'I know what's in there!
It's a fuzzy radio and black and white TV.'
'No, that's not what's in the staffroom.'

'It's a hot jacuzzi and a year's supply of sweets!'
'Yes, that's correct Jessica!
That's what's in the staffroom
And that's why I must go!'

Morag Gillon (9)
Sacred Heart Primary School, Ilkley

IN THE STAFFROOM

Hurry up kids
I wanna get my lunch
And get to the staffroom
What's in there?
What's so special
About it?

A jacuzzi and pool
To calm them down
And Sky TV for free

Once I even saw a spy camera
They are probably all around the school
I think there is a McD's in there
And a dungeon
With children eating lobsters
That's what I think.

Andrew Ettenfield (8)
Sacred Heart Primary School, Ilkley

WHAT'S IN THE STAFFROOM?

There are games in the staffroom
A tombola to win
PlayStation
Chocolate machine
Coffee maker
DVD player
And cool books
Spy televisions
Tea and a kettle
A jacuzzi for fun

Mouldy tea with gone-off milk
A swimming pool with a diving board
To calm teachers down
Cornflakes for breakfast

That's what I think is in a teacher's staffroom.

Jade Davy (8)
Sacred Heart Primary School, Ilkley

ANNA'S TEACHER

My sister told me a story one day
And this is how it started,
On a cold, nippy autumn day
When all the clouds were grey

My sister, Anna, was walking to school,
When she heard a car engine noise,
She thought, 'How could this be
When all the other students walk?'
That's what she told me.

But it was Mr Dude on his dudiecord,
I asked Anna what it meant
But she didn't know either,
But then Anna said to me,
'There was something he said,'
She claimed to be strange
And this is what he said,
'Outa mah way!'
And that is it for today!

Ruth Doherty (8)
Sacred Heart Primary School, Ilkley

MY TEACHER AND LITTLE JANE

There we were, bored and sulking,
The teacher scrabbling on the floor for the board rubber like a rodent,
But Amy had it in her hand.
Annabelle wrote on the board, *Class dismissed*
And everybody went.
'I'm not going,' said quiet little Jane.
'Of course you won't. You're a good girl.
You'll learn much more than them!'
Next day in the spelling test, they got zero, she got 10.

There we were, piled up on top of each other,
Peeking through the creaking door at the spider crawling
Up the teacher's trouser leg.
Teacher's chomping on his chicken and pickle roll,
While spider's on his lap.
'Sir, are you scared of spiders?' said quiet little Jane.
'Of course I'm not. I'm big and fearless.
No spider frightens me!'
'Argh!' he screamed and then went green.

'Help me, Jane, it's in my tea!'

There we are, in the playground,
Teacher stumbles out - 'Since you're still here, take these.'
And hands us our SATs results.
'Here Mum, you look and tell me what I got.'
'Yippee, I got an A.'
'Sir, have you got mine?' said quiet little Jane.
'Of course I have. You got A*. You got much more than them.'

But Mummy says she's proud of me - I'll come back here again!

Helena Below (9)
Sacred Heart Primary School, Ilkley

WHAT TEACHERS DO BEHIND YOUR BACK

Did you know when you turn your back
Teachers stick their tongues out?
And when everyone is silent, 'Fire!' they shout
When everyone is working, they put mud on your shoes
And when all are outside, they throw paper in the loos
And they always mark things wrong
So it won't take as long
And when you go on a school trip
They stay on the coach and make it a tip
It's always teachers who scribble in books
And they only care about their looks
Have you ever heard one say, 'Tidy up.'
Well they're the real messy pups!
Teachers always sneak out to the kitchens to eat
They steal the puddings and leave the meat
Teachers aren't really adults you know
They're little children, like you or me
Blown up like balloons, you see!

Michael Loy (9)
Sacred Heart Primary School, Ilkley

TEACHERS

Teachers talk
Teachers walk
Teachers shout
Teachers count
Teachers read
Teachers lead
Teachers mime
Teachers tell the time
There's nothing else
A teacher can do
Apart from keep a pet puffin
And of course
They can eat a muffin.

Natasha Verspyck (8)
Sacred Heart Primary School, Ilkley

SPORTS

Footie's quite good
Diving's brill
Running's the best
They need skill

Swimming's tiring
Goggles are for hiring
Some people are fast
Some people are slow
You still go

Running's my favourite
It's ace
I've got to go
I've got a race.

Kara Parry (10)
Sacred Heart RC Primary School, Sowerby Bridge

CHOCOLATE

Chocolate is nice, chocolate is good
Chocolate is tasty and the best
Choc makes you feel so good
If you don't like it, we will have a row
Chocolate makes you feel sick
You'll just have to go to the toilet
And be quick
Chocolate is lovely, chocolate is bubbly
Chocolate is the right type for me
I just love it
I'll have it for tea and I'll have it for my supper.

Sarah Cahill
Sacred Heart RC Primary School, Sowerby Bridge

SPACE

Space is the place where aliens dash
And meteorites crash and bash
And the stars gleam so bright
Brighter than the moon on a winter's night
I heard a sound, it sounded like this, *bzzzzzz*
It would not stop all night
I couldn't go to sleep all night.

Callum Rimmer (9)
Sacred Heart RC Primary School, Sowerby Bridge

THE FAIR

The fair is fun,
It makes me feel excited,
You can hear the music playing loud,
As people scream and shout.

I look around from left to right,
Looking for a ride,
Will it be a roller coaster
Twisting high and low
Or will it be a waltzer
Spinning to and fro?

I treat myself to candyfloss,
As I make my way back home,
I haven't got a penny left,
But I've had a really good time.

Daniel Ball (9)
Sacred Heart RC Primary School, Sowerby Bridge

DOUBLE BUBBLES

I come home from school and get in a bubbly bath
It's relaxing, soft and popping mad
I stay in the bath all night with a sweet, amazing cup of tea
When I am in the bath with a sweet-smelling cup of tea
My mum shouts up, 'Time to go to bed!'
But I say,
'What about double bubbles?
I don't want it to go down the plughole.'
When I go to school, I do my work in the stink
With double bubbles,
It's so cool!

Charlie Wilkinson (10)
Sacred Heart RC Primary School, Sowerby Bridge

THEME PARK

I was going to a theme park
It was very dark
I went on a ride and all I did was slide
I got off the ride
We went past bingo
We heard loopy ladies saying,
'Full house'
The loopy lights went on
'Let's go and get some popping popcorn
And see a movie.'

We went to see some Disney characters
Got a stick of sticky rock
But it is just my luck
When I am sick on the crazy corkscrew
Oh no!
I was going bananas when I saw the clown
He turned me upside down
It was just as bad as going on a
High ride
I am on my way home now
Chewing some bubblegum
When I said, *'Hello'* to my brother, Tom
I accidentally dropped gum in his hair

Oops!

Amber Ransley (10)
Sacred Heart RC Primary School, Sowerby Bridge

FORMULA ONE

Here comes Ferrari, *zoom, zoom, zoom!*
Hear its engine, *boom, boom, boom!*
It turns the corner nice and steady
The green light's on, get ready

Look, it's Jaguar, it's coming pretty quick
It's coming so quick, in fact it could break a brick
It turns the corner nice and steady
The green light's on, get ready

McClaren's coming, it's closing in now
Look how fast it's coming, wow!
It turns the corner nice and steady
The green light's on, get ready
Go!

Matthew Carey (10)
Sacred Heart RC Primary School, Sowerby Bridge

FOOTBALL MAD

Football, football, football mad
I am like my big-boned dad
If you saw him you would know
He's just like my football hero

My big-boned dad supports Man U
All my family do too
We've been to matches, game by game
But it's always been the same
My dad jumps up and says, 'What a goal!'
As Nistelrooy does a roll.

Rebecca Kenyon (10)
Sacred Heart RC Primary School, Sowerby Bridge

MY BEST MATE

My best mate is really loud
You can hear him from miles around
My best mate is so cool
He can swim in the 12ft 2
My best mate will never be poor
Even if he lived in the moors
My best mate has a girlfriend
But our friendship will never end
My best mate is so great
He can eat grub when it's out of date
My best mate is really cunning
He can leap while he's running
My best mate hates roller coaster rides
He prays to God, 'Don't let me die!'
My best mate is real sporty
But he's also kind of naughty.

Sean Regan (10)
Sacred Heart RC Primary School, Sowerby Bridge

ANIMALS

H   ippos are so fat
U   mbrella fish are so flat
L   ions are so hungry
L   emurs are so hungry
A   nimals eat pie
B   ats fly
A   crobats do lots of gymnastics
L   ynx do lots of practice
O   strich do lots of running
O   ctopi are so cunning.

Max Brown (9)
Sacred Heart RC Primary School, Sowerby Bridge

HOLIDAYS

Holidays are fun,
They can be mad,
Holidays are amazing,
Especially if you are a lad.

Holidays are so great,
When you play and run around,
You get lots of healthy exercise,
As soon as you hit the ground.

Something else that's fun to do
Is going to the beach,
But if you stay there too long,
You will turn the colour peach.

Ryan Murphy (10)
Sacred Heart RC Primary School, Sowerby Bridge

SPACE

Space is the place where everyone wants to go
Comet flashers, meteor smashers
And my spaceship dashes
Aliens here, aliens there
Aliens everywhere
Men in Black come to kill aliens
But we just came to have some fun
Some people like aliens
Some people don't
Aliens come to invade all day long
They are green, they are blue,
They are bigger than you.
Boo!

David Carter (10)
Sacred Heart RC Primary School, Sowerby Bridge

THE CREEPY WOOD

I walked into a wood
I heard a funny voice
It sent a shiver up my spine
And then I said, 'I feel fine'

I knew very well I wasn't scared
I heard a crack, someone was there
I tiptoed out, I knew I could
And then I fell into a puddle of mud

So I plucked up my courage and plodded on
I heard a scream, what's going on?
Then I looked down at the muddy floor
There in front of me was a weird looking door

My arm was shaking really bad
I lifted my hand and opened the door
'Boo woo hoo' went a ghost
Eating some of his hot buttered toast.

Shannon Horridge (9)
Sacred Heart RC Primary School, Sowerby Bridge

THE ZOO

One day I went to the zoo
It was all hullabaloo
I saw a giraffe, it ate my hat
I saw a monkey, it ate my Crunchie
I saw a bear, it ripped my hair
And then I woke up in bed with my ted.

Colin Millns (10)
Sacred Heart RC Primary School, Sowerby Bridge

CHOCOLATE

Chocolate, what a word
I love fruit and nut
It's my favourite bar of all
But give me any chocolate
And you won't see it at all

We eat it on the sofa
We eat it on the floor
But *beware,* your fingers
Will be chocolaty for evermore

Chocolate, chocolate everywhere
I wish I had chocolate every day
I could eat it for dinner, breakfast too
I wouldn't feel sick or need the loo.

Bethany Leslie (9)
Sacred Heart RC Primary School, Sowerby Bridge

MY FOOTBALL DREAM

As I'm blinking, I am thinking about my football dream,
I wish I could walk into a football stadium and watch my boots gleam.
I wish I could be a footballer and have lots of money,
I wish I could be a footballer and play when it's sunny.
I want to be a footballer to meet other people,
I want to be a footballer and stand as tall as a steeple.
I want to be a footballer so I can drive a shiny car,
I want to be a footballer so I can shine like a star.
I want to be a footballer so I can hear the crowd cheer,
I want to be a footballer so I can be player of the year.

Alex Rhodes (9)
Sacred Heart RC Primary School, Sowerby Bridge

HULLABALOO

Fast, loopy, crazy, crackers
Blowing bubbles, nothing matters
Wild, mad, in the zoo
Please let me go to the loo
Cartoon characters love to laugh
But they get pretty daft

Fast, speedy, zooming, mad
This describes a little lad
This little lad that I know
His name is pretty weird
So let's give it a go
Hullabaloo
Hullabaloo!
Now it's time to take you through a day
In the life of *Hullabaloo!*

Ellie Gerrard (10)
Sacred Heart RC Primary School, Sowerby Bridge

BALLOONS

Balloons make me happy
Flying in the sky
They make me speedy
And very, very crazy
I see colours everywhere
Blue, red, orange and pink
The yellow is bright
And flies high in the sky
It looks like the sun is in my room
But really it is just a balloon.

Amy Leonard (9)
Sacred Heart RC Primary School, Sowerby Bridge

HULLABALOO!

Somebody was coming up the stairs
Thump! Thump! Thump!

Somebody was walking along the corridor
Bump! Bump! Bump!

Somebody was opening the bedroom door
With a *slump* and a *creak!*

Somebody was coming closer and closer,
I started making a *hullabaloo!*

There was more footsteps,
I heard a voice!

Then a scream!
Then a shout!

Creak!

The bedroom light went on
And somebody stood there saying . . .

'What's all this *hullabaloo*?'

It was only me and my mum in the room!

Bethany Horner *(9)*
Sacred Heart RC Primary School, Sowerby Bridge

HULLABALOO

One time I was grounded,
I went out the window,
Just like a mouse I went,
To go and play at my friend's house,
But he was at the park,
So I went to go play with his dog, Spark,
All he said was *bark*,
Then as quick as a flash,
Spark took one great big slash,
My arm was dripping with blood,
I climbed back through the window
And tripped over with one big thud,
When my mum heard me she was on the loo,
She slammed the bedroom door wide open
And let out a loud, tremendous, 'What's all this hullabaloo?'

Darrell Bingham (9)
Sacred Heart RC Primary School, Sowerby Bridge

WHERE IS HULLABALOO?

Hullabaloo is the one with a clue,
Hullabaloo has got the flu.

Hullabaloo is tall and round,
Hullabaloo makes a great sound.

Hullabaloo is on the ride,
Hullabaloo down at the tide.

Hullabaloo is crazy and cool,
Hullabaloo is in the pool.

Hullabaloo is up to tricks,
So watch out before he *flicks!*

Kerry Lister (9)
Sacred Heart RC Primary School, Sowerby Bridge

WHAT IS HULLABALOO?

Hullabaloo is big baboons
Hullabaloo is flying balloons

Hullabaloo is the playground's noise
Hullabaloo is kids with toys

Hullabaloo is kids wanting sweets
Hullabaloo is kids wanting treats

Hullabaloo is all your dreams
Hullabaloo is flavoured ice creams

Hullabaloos is kids being loud
Hullabaloo is a mega sound

Hullabaloo is kids being wild
Hullabaloo is an energetic child.

That's what hullabaloo is!

Lili Cordingley (8)
Sacred Heart RC Primary School, Sowerby Bridge

HULLABALOO

I have a blue leg but a green head,
It is a strange thing but it can be true,
I have a red leg, but a pink arm too,
My mum thinks it's strange,
But my brother thinks it's cool,
Some people think I'm a *monster,*
My name is Hullabaloo!

Nathaniel Powell (8)
Sacred Heart RC Primary School, Sowerby Bridge

HULLABALOO, ALL THINGS BLUE!

The sea and sky are blue,
So are cars and paper too.

Felt pens and pencils are blue,
So are book covers and rulers too.

T-shirts and flowers are blue,
So are butterflies and gel pens too.

Hats and handbags are blue,
So are pencil cases and boxes too.

Clocks and purses are blue,
So are cushions and teddies too.

Umbrellas and rucksacks are blue,
So are carpets and balls too.

Counters and picture frames are blue,
So are rubbers and raindrops too.

Blue, blue, blue,
Blue, blue, blue.

Lucy Mitchell (8)
Sacred Heart RC Primary School, Sowerby Bridge

NIGHT CINQUAIN

Night-time
It's really dark
Hear voices all around
Shadows creeping on my ceiling
Freaky!

Kane Booker (10)
Sutton CP School

NIGHT

Dogs bark
Wolves howl
Shadows form
Creepy

Foxes come
Out at night
To find their prey
What a fright

Badgers out
Black and white
But watch out
They do bite!

Thomas Ogden (11)
Sutton CP School

EARTHQUAKE!

A roaring bear,
A pounding drum,
A concrete cracker,
A deadly criminal,
A wall demolisher,
A rule breaker.

Robert Berry (11)
Sutton CP School

NIGHT

Stars shine
The staircase creaks
Foxes hunt for their prey
The tap dripping in the bathroom
Night ends

Clocks tick
Muffling voices
The owls start hooting
Badgers rustle through the bushes
I stare.

Samantha Harrison (10)
Sutton CP School

I'M SCARED!

Heart beating,
Stopped breathing,
Owls hooting,
Badgers snuffling.

Floorboards creaking,
Hands fidgeting,
People snoring,
Stars glistening.

Isn't night freaky?

Abigail Lorimer (10)
Sutton CP School

SKY

A cloud carrier
A rain bringer
A rainbow wearer
A blue sea
A protective cover
An aeroplane playground.

Chris Raine (10)
Sutton CP School

A FACE AT THE WINDOW

A face at the window
I think my bed is made of sticky dough
As I look from my bed
Beginning to dread
Just thinking about it makes me twitch
As I reach for the light switch
I'm safe again thanks to the light
But tomorrow I'll just hold on tight.

Simon Hargraves (10)
Sutton CP School

NIGHT-TIME

Owls hooting
Midnight calling
Shadows creeping over my ceiling
It's night-time
Children go to sleep
Trees rustling.

Thomas Wood (11)
Sutton CP School

SCHOOL

If you can answer hard questions
And a straightened face,
If you can write a story,
Without a spelling mistake,
If you can do work neatly
And draw a picture too,
If you can have a break time,
Without having to stand in the hall,
If you can sit through assembly,
Without talking to the person next to you,
Then you are a pupil at Sutton CP School,
My friend!

Katy Stares (10)
Sutton CP School

NIGHT-TIME

Shadows creak
Owls peep
Stars shine
Through the chill of my spine
Crunched leaves
Upon a thousand trees.

Emma Greenwood (10)
Sutton CP School

THE OWLS' WAY

They hoot and fly over hilltops
You can't hear them overhead
You can try and listen to their flutters
But their wings sound completely dead

We can look inside the forest
We can look inside the wood
It will take ages and ages to find one
Because they're as sly as Robin Hood

The owls are the ultimate night prowler
They'll thrash their prey so fast
Your heart will pump like lightning
They're the devils of the past!

Joseph Robertshaw (11)
Sutton CP School

FREEZING

F   luttering snowflakes flying down.
R   ed robins jumping up and down.
E   verybody playing in the snow.
E   vening hours come so soon.
Z   ipping up big winter coats.
I   cicles forming on the roof.
N   othing can stop the snow from falling.
G   etting up to see the snow falling on the ground.

Daniel Wild (11)
Sutton CP School

MIDNIGHT

At midnight the clock strikes,
Owls hoot,
People snore,
Leaves rustle.

At midnight the moon glows,
Hearts jump,
People shiver,
Cars bump.

At midnight the washer spins,
Mice run,
Foxes dig,
Badgers sniff.

At daytime people wake,
Badgers sleep,
Hunters shoot,
Cars beep!

James Smith (11)
Sutton CP School

SKUNK

Bush rustler
Scent leaver
Fierce hunter
Worm eater
Stripy back.

Daniel Hart (11)
Sutton CP School

STORM AT BEDTIME

Trees rustle,
Rain bangs;
Stars shine,
Sheets hang.

Clocks tick,
Shadows creep;
Hedgehogs shuffle,
Rats peep.

Ghosts haunt,
Stairs creak;
Curtains blow,
Drains leak.

Voices muffle,
Lightning flashes;
Bushes thrash,
Thunder crashes.

Katie Booker (11)
Sutton CP School

DARKNESS CINQUAIN

Night-time,
The moon appears,
Darkness is all over,
A dark black fog everywhere,
Midnight.

Daniel Longbottom (11)
Sutton CP School

IN THE DEAD OF THE NIGHT

Your heart jumps
The stairs creak
The gate opens
And shadows peep

Your dad snores
The badgers hunt
The windows freeze
And hedgehogs grunt

Your curtains move
The floorboards rumble
The bushes whistle
And voices mumble

At night!

Jack Barraclough (11)
Sutton CP School

SCARED IN THE NIGHT CINQUAINS

You're scared,
I know you are,
Strange shadows in the dark,
You're hiding under your covers,
Creepy.

Still scared,
Moon is shining,
Flapping sheets look like ghosts,
Doors are creaking in the hallway,
Help me!

Isobel Sutcliffe (10)
Sutton CP School

Fox

The foxes prowl into the night
To look for a lonely field
He fights the sheep like a knight
But the sheep don't have a shield

He sticks his teeth into the flesh
Of the poor and lonely sheep
The sheep gets stuck in the wire mesh
And then the farmer begins to creep

The fox hears a gunshot in the midnight sky
And he hears the farmer's door
The sheep lets out a fearful cry
But the fox is there no more.

Matthew Burton (10)
Sutton CP School

Night-Time Noises

Floorboards creaking,
Clock ticking,
Leaves rustling,
Tap dripping.

Owls hooting,
Hedgehogs snuffling,
Muffled voices,
Footsteps shuffling.

What was that?
Lying there . . . chill,
Can't do anything,
Lie there . . . still!

Sarah Liu (11)
Sutton CP School

NOISES AT NIGHT

Stars twinkle
Moon shining
Trees rustling
Hedgehogs snuffling

People sleeping
Stairs creaking
Tap dripping
Radiator trickling

Owls hooting
Quiet voices
Bats flapping
Here comes morning.

Lottie Hicks (10)
Sutton CP School

GHOST

Ghosts lurk in the shadows
Trapdoors in the floor
Creaking doors in the corridor
Phantom organs playing
Headless spectors in the wardrobe
Mummies in their tombs
Massive spiders in their webs
Worms in the kitchen tap
Witches by the fireplace
Frogs and flies on a silver plate
Thunder starts to boom
The moon is born
The sun is dead
And soon you'll be dead too.

Chris Riley (11)
Sutton CP School

MONSTER

His large jaws
Give him character,
His snarling eyes
Give his frightening look,
His blunt teeth
Give chills down your spine,
His bitten ears
Don't help a bit,
His bearded chin
Gives attention to his grin,
His upturned nose
Sniffs out his foes,
His scruffy hair
Could kill a bear,
His angry eyebrows
Express his anger,
Dead!

Sam Harrison (10)
Sutton CP School

NIGHT CINQUAIN

At night,
I lay awake,
I wonder what's outside,
Something is creeping round my room,
I scream . . .

Charlotte McPike (10)
Sutton CP School

PROWLER

While owls awake and badgers stir
And wander round the hill,
A lowly screeching fills the air,
The prowler starts to kill.

The prowler wanders round the farm,
Slowly closing in,
He disappears into the night,
To answer to his kin.

He runs along the waving fields
And pounces on his prey,
He stands alert as footsteps sound
And sleeps throughout the day.

A light surrounds him, gunshots sound,
The prowler lies down low,
What happened to him in the night?
No one will ever know.

Findley Harrison (11)
Sutton CP School

ALONE AT NIGHT

I'm alone at night
My mum's gone out
I turn my music loud
My mum comes home
I'm not alone.

Lynsey Vincent (11)
Sutton CP School

MIDNIGHT SCARES CINQUAIN

Clocks tick,
Stars in the sky,
Heard laughter from downstairs,
Howling from outside my window,
What's that?

Bethany Ellison (10)
Sutton CP School

HOMEWORK HAIKU

Have we got homework?
Because I like the homework,
I have finished it.

Christina Foster (11)
Upper Whitley JI School

SUMMER HAIKU

Summer is soon here,
Sea, sun, sand and holidays,
What seasonal fun.

Daniel Archer (10)
Upper Whitley JI School

WINTER, SUMMER HAIKUS

Winter is so cold
Colder than all the others
Come on, snowball fight

Summer is so warm
Warmer than all the others
Come on, let's sunbathe.

James Clarkson (9)
Upper Whitley JI School

THE ANCIENT CASTLE

The ancient castle,
Once a battleground,
Gigantic, magnificent, indestructible,
Like a stone giant,
As old as a dinosaur,
It makes me feel minute,
As small as a germ,
The ancient castle,
It shows what we can do when we work together.

Thomas Sowerby (9)
Upper Whitley JI School

WINTER HAIKU

Brrr, it's cold out here,
Snowflakes falling on the ground,
Christmas will be soon.

Rachel Adams (10)
Upper Whitley JI School

SWEETS

Sweets are eaten fast
Time goes whizzing past
It's time to go
No time to show
My lovely crunching Mars bar

Hear my *munch*
And *crunch, crunch, crunch*
Eat it slow
And go, go, go

I've eaten it all
And now I'm tall
My lovely crunching Mars bar.

Jamie Holmes (10)
Upper Whitley JI School

MY BEST FRIEND

My best friend,
Working hard all day,
Hard-working, smart and kind,
Like a brain in a box,
Like somebody who copies me,
Really old and she's very young,
My best friend,
We're really smart together.

Emily Stalmach (8)
Upper Whitley JI School

WATER SPLASHES HAIKU

Water splashes down,
Raindrops on the patio,
No sunbathing now.

Dale Jones (9)
Upper Whitley JI School

PUPPIES HAIKU

Puppies at my house
They look so cute and cuddly
Miss them when they go.

Lisa Bentley (9)
Upper Whitley JI School

AUTUMN HAIKU

Autumn leaves falling,
Forming together a hill,
Inside . . . a hedgehog.

Whitney-Jayne Boswell (9)
Upper Whitley JI School

SEASONAL HAIKUS

Spring
Buds full, fat and green
Pink blossoms trembling on trees
The warm breath of spring

Summer
Hi sun, big and bright
Shining your rays down on me
Filling me with glee

Autumn
A flurry of wind
Blows leaves off a big black tree
Autumn is now here

Winter
Snowflakes are falling
Running off the big bare trees
Snowman on the path.

Luke Archer (8)
Upper Whitley JI School

GHOULS

My first ghoul is a zombie
All green, black and red

My second is a ghost
Extraordinarily hard to see

My third ghoul is Frankenstein
Realistic but dead

My fourth is my shadow
And he is always following me!

Megan McKay (10)
Upper Whitley JI School

ANIMALS

1 for a tiger,
2 for a cat,
3 for a fish,
4 for a rat,
5 for a kangaroo,
6 for a seal,
7 for a crocodile,
8 for an eel,
9 for a sheep,
10 for a leopard,
11 for a snake,
12 for a shepherd.

Katie Wilson (8)
Upper Whitley JI School

ONE, TWO, THREE, ANIMAL STREET

One for a dog,
Two for a cat,
Three for a bird,
Four for a rat,
Five for a bee,
Six for a lead,
Seven for a vet,
Eight for in need,
Nine for a fly,
Ten for a hen,
Eleven for a spider,
Twelve in a den.

Naomi Bamforth (8)
Upper Whitley JI School

LITTER

Cola cans,
Crisp packets,
Smelly apples
And cloth rags.

Dog dirt,
Jam jars,
Newspapers
And plastic bags.

I'm fed up
With all this litter,
Can't somebody clear it up?

It's got to be soon,
It's got to be quicker,
Hurry up
Or we'll have blown our chance.

Jodie Cork-Dove (9)
Wellington Primary School

THE GARDENER

I speak to him, no answer back,
So I'm forced to keep to the country track.

He digs away the dandelions, so yellow,
But I can't help feeling sorry for the fellow.

He slaves away relentlessly and never fails,
Through thunder, rainfall, frost and hail.

The gorse, the heather, the blossom in the trees,
How he tramps through the grass in the stinging breeze.

Up the wall the ivy scrambles,
Along with the twigs and the holly and brambles.

The lilies are floating in the trickling stream,
While he feeds the birds through the sun's golden gleam.

He waters the plants and the flowers that bloom,
As I watch that lone figure from up in my room.

Summer arrives, the best time of year
And long dreary days at last disappear.

After a long, but fruitful day,
With a satisfied glow, he trudges away.

Chloe Sutcliffe (11)
Wellington Primary School

PLANET JUPITER

We didn't see aliens
On planet Jupiter
But we saw
Where the aliens had been

We saw blue snot
That was dripping
Off burnt trees

We saw scaly skin
That the alien had left behind
It was sticky
With blood dripping down it

We saw dead bodies
That were burnt
To the bone

We saw sticky blood
From dead bodies
It looked awful

We didn't see aliens
On planet Jupiter
But we had evidence
That aliens were living.

Jessica Fisher (9)
Wellington Primary School

ALIEN FORTRESS

We never saw aliens but we did see evidence of them,
We saw alien spines hung on branches,
We saw rolled-up dung, but we never saw aliens.

We saw aliens' slimy fingers scattered on the ground,
We saw alien bogies,
We saw a giant tooth all covered in blood,
An alien body with no insides left.

We saw an alien leg being ripped up,
We saw half-eaten eyes still bleeding and it really made you throw up,
We saw a half-eaten space buggy with blood all over it
And empty astronaut suits covered in blood.

We saw half-eaten food blocks,
We saw scaly skin that made you shiver down your back,
We saw half-eaten arms that made you shiver down your spine,
We saw evidence of aliens, now I am believing.

Andrew Shanley (9)
Wellington Primary School

PLANET MERCURY

We didn't see aliens on planet Mercury
But we saw where the aliens had been

We saw half-eaten books written in a language I didn't understand
We saw fruit pink, blue and red

We saw alien droppings which stunk like burnt-out cigars

We saw guns, bombs and evil plans
To destroy planet Earth

We saw half-eaten shuttles
With dead astronauts inside

We didn't see aliens on planet Mercury
But we got the closest we'd ever be.

Bradley Marsden (8)
Wellington Primary School

PLANET BUMPY HUMPY LAND

We didn't see aliens
On Bumpy Humpy Land
But we saw
Where the aliens had been

We saw alien skin
Bubbling in red-hot lava
A chunk of alien fur
Stuck to a snotty tissue

We saw human fingers
With their names painted on them
They were stuck in the ground

We saw blood running
Down the trees
A rocket had a dead person in it
Without a head

We didn't see aliens
On planet Bumpy Humpy Land
But we knew that something lived there!

Sarah Davidson (8)
Wellington Primary School

PLANET MARS

We didn't see aliens
On planet Mars
But we saw
Where the aliens had been

We saw alien dung
On a cold stone
That was smelling of raw fish
That made you want to faint

We saw small alien trolleys
That were bent in the corner
And had alien wrappers on them

We saw alien money
With pictures of their kings and queens
That was scattered in craters

We saw alien graveyards
With eyes, ears and arms sticking out
With a head poking out of the ground
Aliens' slimy skin
Hanging from branches
And dripping with blood

We didn't see aliens on planet Mars
But we found evidence
That aliens lived there.

Lewis Ragan (9)
Wellington Primary School

MARS COMPARED TO EARTH

We didn't see aliens
On planet Mars,
But we saw where
The aliens had been.

We saw alien tracks
In boiling hot lava
That was bubbling over
Red landscape.

We saw ray guns
Scattered on the wax-like ground
And laser beams
Shooting out of them.

We saw crashed spaceships
With flames licking out
Of the engines.

We saw alien food
That was purple
And thrown all over the ground.

We didn't see aliens on planet Mars
But we knew that they were there.

James Emmett (9)
Wellington Primary School

ALIEN FOREST

We didn't see aliens on planet Mars
But we saw where the aliens had been

We saw slimy scaly fingers hanging from branch to branch
With long grey nails on the slimy hand

We saw massive blue sparkly footprints
That were bigger than 70 elephants' feet put together

We saw tiny dead aliens that had been eaten
By fearsome large creatures

We saw huge half-eaten legs with gigantic teeth marks in them
We saw scraggy hair hanging from a huge tree
That had spiders crawling on it

We didn't see aliens on planet Mars
But now we've seen evidence we can believe.

Abigail Hirst (9)
Wellington Primary School

ZULO, ZULO

We didn't see aliens on planet Zulo
But we saw where the aliens had been

We saw sick where a poorly alien had been
On a lonely Zulo night

We saw a gigantic rock where the master was living
And telling everyone what to do

We saw ripped-up films and broken cameras on the rocks

We saw bones with goo on them
And they had been half-eaten

We saw a science lab where they had been working out
How to act like humans

We saw tracks heading towards the master's home
By dinosaur-like things

We didn't see aliens on Zulo
But we believed that there was life.

Sam McMahon (9)
Wellington Primary School

SCHOOL RULES

Don't forget to change your book
Mrs Dixon is sure to look

You will break a golden rule
If you go running through the school

Be sure to tidy your desk
Then you will be the best

You should never bring sweets to school
It will make the others drool

If you should turn up late
You'll get an inappropriate

To these rules you should adhere
Or Mrs Wood will punish you severe.

James Archer (9)
Wellington Primary School

GOOD SOUNDS

With a *bang* and a *crash*
Mum's not home
Let's party with a garden gnome
Everybody gather round
Let's make a wicked, awesome sound

The kitchen is a good place
For sounds and things to crash together
Who gives a care about the weather?
The sitting room has got vases
Broken ones
Oops!

Joel Harrison (9)
Westville House School

THE GREAT DREAM

As I lay here, sleeping in my bed,
I saw some pictures in my head.

I saw the forests being burnt,
After this, I had learnt,

That we should not burn down wood,
For the purpose of no good.

We use the space to make highways,
Being used every day.

Killing wildlife by the score,
Encouraging pollution more and more.

Suddenly I had a thought,
We should not have brought

Great big, whopping saws,
Breaking the good forestry laws.

I realised I must do something fast,
Our forests were under attack!

So I called upon Mr Brainpower,
To help stop men killing every flower!

As I lie here, thinking in my head,
I can't help to wonder,
Is every forest dead?

Jennifer Caisley (8)
Westville House School

MY WONDERLAND

I live in a wonderland
Where all is covered with sweets and sand
The trees are made from marshmallows
The grass is coloured with different yellows
The stones are made from chocolate
Quick or I'll be late!
I've got an appointment with my marshmallow mate
Oh, about him, he's quite funny
And he's got a pet, a little bunny
The bunny is red, blue and white
It really is quite a sight
He hops around
And makes a sound
You would think he'd never make
He eats marshmallows
And his room is grass yellows
It's all quite strange for heaven's sake
My marshmallow mate, he's got a mate
His mate is made from chocolate
His chocolate mate has got a mate
And he is made from liquorice
In fact all his house is made from it
He licks the walls and the chair
Oh, and the stair
And he has a mate, a pineapple mate
And he is always late, late, late
That is the end of my wonderland
Where all is covered with sweets and sand
Bye and hope you visit soon
Oh and PS, the pineapple mate has a pet baboon!

Jessica Peppiate (9)
Westville House School

IF I WERE MAGIC

If I were magic
I would change the school
Into a giant swimming pool

I would change the world
Into a place of fun
And play rugby with everyone

I would eat sweets
And nothing else
And share them with my friends

It has been a tiring day
But nothing will go away
Because in the morning
I will still be
Magic!

Daniel Jeffrey (9)
Westville House School

MUSIC

I like bells, you ring them up and down.
I like bells at Christmas time.
How they make a sound like *ding-dong*.
I have a bell at home, I ring it
And make a noisy sound.
Bells are big and small,
Their colours are gold,
A pretty brass gold.
People ring bells at church,
You pull on a rope
And make it go *ding-dong*.

Sophie Patchett (8)
Westville House School

My Bunny Rabbit

I love my bunny rabbit
Because he's really fluffy
He's softer than a teddy bear

My rabbit's a real softy
He's cute and real friendly
He's a real big thing too

He's a browny-gold colour
With soft paws
But I'll always love him, however sharp the claws

He's got long ears and always peers
And never has a fear
I love to be near him

I call him a fur ball
Because he is covered in fur
But I love him still
Because he's Hank.

Lydia Holloway (8)
Westville House School

THE GARDEN GNOME

There is a magical person in my garden,
He does the damage but never says pardon.
He lives by the pond,
Of which he's very fond.
Who is he? He is the gnome.

He tips the dustbin upside down,
But all my dad does is frown.
He would raid the house if he could,
But he can't he is the size of a mouse.
Who is he? He is the garden gnome.

My mum wants to execute him,
But I want to forgive his sin
And my dad wants to forgive him
And put him in the bin.
Though my cat would just chase him.
Who is he? He is the garden gnome.

James Smith (9)
Westville House School

MAGIC DREAMS

The magic inside my head at night
Begins when I turn off my bedside light.

I snuggle into my cosy bed
And magic dreams begin in my head.

I dream of lands and faraway places,
With lots of people with smiley faces.

Horses and ponies in green lush grass,
Galloping, trotting, free and fast.

Trees are swaying from side to side,
Water flowing and rives that glide.

I dream of being a bird that flies,
Free and fast in endless skies.

Dreams are weird,
Dreams are strange.

But there is one thing I wouldn't change,
The magic dreams in my head that come out every night.

Chloe Moss (8)
Westville House School

THE DEEP DARK HOLE

I was walking along the street
And suddenly I fell down a hole
At the bottom, it was very, very dark
I found a track heading for the west
I started going down the green, disgusting track

Suddenly I saw a very ugly monster
I started walking back very slowly
And he started walking slowly
Then I ran as fast as I could
Then he ran as fast as he could
I finally found the hole that I fell down
I tried to get out but it was too far up
The monster was catching up
I finally got up before he caught me.

Alexander Rose (8)
Westville House School

MY PET

I have a pet
Who always gets wet
Her name is Betty Boo
She plays with sticks
Her paws she licks
Chases the rabbits all day long
Until the sun goes *bong*
Betty Boo is a dog
And always goes for a jog
She is very greedy too
Betty Boo chases sheep
She does not like the sound *beep*.

Edward Hardy (8)
Westville House School

NATURE AWAY FROM US

I really like nature
Especially in the sea
All the fish that live in there
I think have a lucky life
The sharks rule the area
So do the whales
Especially the killer whales
All the animals that crawl the floor
Including the lobsters, crabs, the lot
They all have great fun
In the ocean

I really like nature
Especially in Kenya
All the animals have to be aware of the poachers
That lurk in the area
Especially the elephants
They want all the tusks
The tigers, they want all their fur
They keep the cubs in a cave
The rhinos are very dangerous
Especially when they're disturbed.

William Shelton (9)
Westville House School

MY CATS

I have two cats called Jasper and Jaffa
One's quite clever but the other's a nutter
They go out at night and catch mice and rats
And come in and scoff from their bowls

Sometimes they sleep all day
Then they get up and play
They go out at night and have a fight with a fox
They come home with it in a box
That poor old fox

They go to the kitchen
Miaow all day
Until it pays off
Food, hooray!

Jonathan McGurk (9)
Westville House School

MUSIC

I like playing the trumpet,
It makes a funny sound,
It sounds like an elephant,
Playing through its nose!

I like playing the trumpet,
It makes a silly sound,
Like an enormous horse,
Neighing in its field!

I like playing the trumpet,
It makes a sort of sound,
It sounds like music
In an orchestra!

Philip Hydleman (8)
Westville House School

MIRACLE LAND

In a house so far away,
Lives a chocolate man who used to say,
'I have a house,
A pineapple house.'
Which he eats away,
He has a bed made from marshmallows, bounce,
The people there are miracle makers,
Some are also bakers.
The schools are made from jelly babies,
The desks aren't made from clay,
But from jelly beans.
Look, the trees are made from liquorice
And the leaves are lollies.
The horses fly and so do the cats
And the dogs rule the land.
People come from far and near to see this miracle land,
So if you go to this miracle land, I should suggest you bring a camera!

Roselle Hirst (9)
Westville House School